PENPALS
for
Handwriting

Year 2 Teacher's Book
(6–7 years)

Gill Budgell   Kate Ruttle

Series Consultants
Sue Palmer   Professor Rhona Stainthorp

Contents

CAMBRIDGE **HITACHI**

www.cambridge-hitachi.com

Scope and sequence

Foundation 1 / 3–5 years

DEVELOPING GROSS MOTOR SKILLS
1 The vocabulary of movement
2 Large movements
3 Responding to music

DEVELOPING FINE MOTOR SKILLS
4 Hand and finger play
5 Making and modelling
6 Links to art
7 Using one-handed tools and equipment

DEVELOPING PATTERNS AND BASIC LETTER MOVEMENTS
8 Pattern-making
9 Responding to music
10 Investigating straight line patterns
11 Investigating loops
12 Investigating circles
13 Investigating angled patterns
14 Investigating eights and spirals

Foundation 2 / Primary 1

Term 2
1 Introducing long ladder letters: *l, i, t, u, j, y*
2 Practising long ladder letters: *l, i*
3 Practising long ladder letters: *t, u*
4 Practising long ladder letters: *j, y*
5 Practising all the long ladder letters
6 Introducing one-armed robot letters: *r, b, n, h, m, k, p*
7 Practising one-armed robot letters: *b, n*
8 Practising one-armed robot letters: *h, m*
9 Practising one-armed robot letters: *k, p*
10 Practising all the one-armed robot letters
11 Introducing capitals for one-armed robot letters: *R, B, N, H, M, K, P*
12 Introducing capitals for long ladder letters: *L, I, T, U, J, Y*

Term 3
13 Introducing curly caterpillar letters: *c, a, d, o, s, g, q, e, f*
14 Practising curly caterpillar letters: *a, d*
15 Practising curly caterpillar letters: *o, s*
16 Practising curly caterpillar letters: *g, q*
17 Practising curly caterpillar letters: *e, f*
18 Practising all the curly caterpillar letters
19 Introducing zig-zag monster letters: *z, v, w, x*
20 Practising zig-zag monster letters: *v, w, x*
21 Introducing capitals for curly caterpillar letters: *C, A, D, O, S, G, Q, E, F*
22 Introducing capitals for zig-zag monster letters: *Z, V, W, X*
23 Exploring *ch, th* and *sh*

Year 1 / Primary 2

Term 1
1 Letter formation practice: long ladder family
2 Letter formation practice: one-armed robot family
3 Letter formation practice: curly caterpillar family
4 Letter formation practice: zig-zag monster family
5 Practising the vowels: *i*
6 Practising the vowels: *u*
7 Practising the vowels: *a*
8 Practising the vowels: *o*
9 Practising the vowels: *e*
10 Letter formation practice: capital letters

Term 2
11 Introducing diagonal join to ascender: joining *at, all*
12 Practising diagonal join to ascender: joining *th*
13 Practising diagonal join to ascender: joining *ch*
14 Practising diagonal join to ascender: joining *cl*
15 Introducing diagonal join, no ascender: joining *in, im*
16 Practising diagonal join, no ascender: joining *cr, tr, dr*
17 Practising diagonal join, no ascender: joining *lp, mp*
18 Introducing diagonal join, no ascender, to an anticlockwise letter: joining *id, ig*
19 Practising diagonal join, no ascender, to an anticlockwise letter: joining *nd, ld*
20 Practising diagonal join, no ascender, to an anticlockwise letter: joining *ng*

Term 3
21 Practising diagonal join, no ascender: joining *ee*
22 Practising diagonal join, no ascender: joining *ai, ay*
23 Practising diagonal join, no ascender: joining *ime, ine*
24 Introducing horizontal join, no ascender: joining *op, oy*
25 Practising horizontal join, no ascender: joining *one, ome*
26 Introducing horizontal join, no ascender, to an anticlockwise letter: joining *oa, og*
27 Practising horizontal join, no ascender, to an anticlockwise letter: joining *wa, wo*
28 Introducing horizontal join to ascender: joining *ol, ot*
29 Practising horizontal join to ascender: joining *wh, oh*
30 Introducing horizontal and diagonal joins to ascender, to an anticlockwise letter: joining *of, if*
31 Assessment

Year 2 / Primary 3

Term 1
1 How to join in a word: high-frequency words
2 Introducing the break letters: *j, g, x, y, z, b, f, p, q, r, s*
3 Practising diagonal join to ascender in words: *eel, eet*
4 Practising diagonal join, no ascender, in words: *a_e*
5 Practising diagonal join, no ascender, to an anticlockwise letter in words: *ice, ide*
6 Practising horizontal join, no ascender, in words: *ow, ou*
7 Practising horizontal join, no ascender, in words: *oy, oi*
8 Practising horizontal join, no ascender, to an anticlockwise letter in words: *oa, ode*
9 Practising horizontal join to ascender in words: *ole, obe*
10 Practising horizontal join to ascender in words: *ook, ool*

Term 2
11 Practising diagonal join to r: *ir, ur, er*
12 Practising horizontal join to r: *or, oor*
13 Introducing horizontal join from r to ascender: *url, irl, irt*
14 Introducing horizontal join from r: *ere*
15 Practising joining to and from r: *air*
16 Introducing diagonal join to s: *dis*
17 Introducing horizontal join to s: *ws*
18 Introducing diagonal join from s to ascender: *sh*
19 Introducing diagonal join from s, no ascender: *si, su, se, sp, sm*
20 Introducing horizontal join from r to an anticlockwise letter: *rs*

Term 3
21 Practising diagonal join to an anticlockwise letter: *ea, ear*
22 Introducing horizontal join to and from f to ascender: *ft, fl*
23 Introducing horizontal join from f, no ascender: *fu, fr*
24 Introducing *qu* (diagonal join, no ascender)
25 Introducing *rr* (horizontal join, no ascender)
26 Introducing *ss* (diagonal join, no ascender, to an anticlockwise letter)
27 Introducing *ff* (horizontal join to ascender)
28 Capital letter practice: height of ascenders and capitals
29 Assessment
30 Assessment

Scope and sequence

Year 3/Primary 4

Term 1
1 Revising joins in a word: long vowel phonemes
2 Revising joins in a word: *le*
3 Revising joins in a word: *ing*
4 Revising joins in a word: high-frequency words
5 Revising joins in a word: new vocabulary
6 Revising joins in a word: *un, de*
7 Revising joins to and from s: *dis*
8 Revising joins to and from r: *re, pre*
9 Revising joins to and from f: *ff*
10 Revising joins: *qu*

Term 2
11 Introducing joining b and p: diagonal join, no ascender, *bi, bu, pi, pu*
12 Practising joining b and p: diagonal join, no ascender, to an anticlockwise letter, *ba, bo, pa, po*
13 Practising joining b and p: diagonal join to ascender, *bl, ph*
14 Relative sizes of letters: silent letters
15 Parallel ascenders: high-frequency words
16 Parallel descenders: adding *y* to words
17 Relative size and consistency: *ly, less, ful*
18 Relative size and consistency: capitals
19 Speed and fluency practice: *er, est*
20 Speed and fluency practice: opposites

Term 3
21 Consistency in spacing: *mis, anti, ex*
22 Consistency in spacing: *non, co*
23 Consistency in spacing: apostrophes
24 Layout, speed and fluency practice: address
25 Layout, speed and fluency practice: dialogue
26 Layout, speed and fluency practice: poem
27 Layout, speed and fluency practice: letter
28 Handwriting style
29 Assessment
30 Handwriting style

Year 4/Primary 5

Term 1
1 Revising joins in a word: *ness, ship*
2 Revising joins in a word: *ing, ed*
3 Revising joins in a word: *s*
4 Revising joins in a word: *ify*
5 Revising joins in a word: *nn, mm, ss*
6 Revising parallel ascenders: *tt, ll, bb*
7 Revising parallel ascenders and descenders: *pp, ff*
8 Revising joins to an anticlockwise letter: *cc, dd*
9 Revising break letters: alphabetical order
10 Linking spelling and handwriting: related words

Term 2
11 Introducing sloped writing
12 Parallel ascenders: *al, ad, af*
13 Parallel descenders and break letters: *ight, ough*
14 Size, proportion and spacing: *ious*
15 Size, proportion and spacing: *able, ful*
16 Size, proportion and spacing: *fs, ves*
17 Speed and fluency: abbreviations for notes
18 Speed and fluency: notemaking
19 Speed and fluency: drafting
20 Speed and fluency: lists

Term 3
21 Size, proportion and spacing: *v, k*
22 Size, proportion and spacing: *ic, ist*
23 Size, proportion and spacing: *ion*
24 Size, proportion and spacing: contractions
25 Speed and fluency: *ible, able*
26 Speed and fluency: diminutives
27 Print alphabet
28 Print capitals
29 Assessment
30 Presentational skills: font styles

Years 5 & 6/Primary 6 & 7

Year 5 Handwriting
1 Revision: practising sloped writing
2 Revision: practising the joins
3 Developing style for speed: joining from *t*
4 Developing style for speed: looping from *g, j* and *y*
5 Developing style for speed: joining from *f*
6 Developing style for speed: joining from *s*
7 Developing style for speed: writing *v, w, x* and *z* at speed
8 Developing style for speed: pen breaks in longer words
9 Different styles for different purposes
10 Assessment

Year 5 Project work
11 Haiku project: making notes
12 Haiku project: organising ideas
13 Haiku project: producing a draft
14 Haiku project: publishing the haiku
15 Haiku project: evaluation
16 Letter project: making notes
17 Letter project: structuring an argument
18 Letter project: producing a draft
19 Letter project: publishing a letter
20 Letter project: evaluation

Year 6 Handwriting
21 Self-assessment: evaluating handwriting
22 Self-assessment: checking the joins
23 Self-assessment: consistency of size
24 Self-assessment: letters resting on baseline
25 Self-assessment: ascenders and descenders
26 Self-assessment: consistency of size of capitals and ascenders
27 Writing at speed: inappropriate closing of letters
28 Writing at speed: identifying unclosed letters
29 Writing at speed: spacing within words
30 Writing at speed: spacing between words

Year 6 Project work
31 Playscript project: collecting information
32 Playscript project: recording ideas
33 Playscript project: producing a draft
34 Playscript project: publishing a playscript
35 Playscript project: evaluation
36 Information notice project: collecting and organising information
37 Information notice project: organising information
38 Information notice project: producing a draft
39 Information notice project: publishing a notice
40 Information notice project: evaluation

Even in this computer-literate age, good handwriting remains fundamental to our children's educational achievement. *Penpals for Handwriting* will help you teach children to develop fast, fluent, legible handwriting. The rationale for introducing joining is fully explained on page 11. This carefully structured handwriting scheme can also make a difference to overall attainment in writing.

Traditional principles in the contemporary classroom

We believe that:

1 A flexible, fluent and legible handwriting style empowers children to write with confidence and creativity. This is an entitlement that needs skilful teaching.
2 Handwriting is a developmental process with its own distinctive stages of sequential growth. We have identified five stages that form the basic organisational structure of *Penpals*:
    1 Readiness for handwriting; gross and fine motor skills leading to letter formation (Foundation / 3–5 years)
    2 Beginning to join (Key Stage 1 / 5–7 years)
    3 Securing the joins (Key Stage 1 and lower Key Stage 2 / 5–9 years)
    4 Practising speed and fluency (lower Key Stage 2 / 7–9 years)
    5 Presentation skills (upper Key Stage 2 / 10–11 years)
3 Handwriting must be actively taught; this can be done in association with spelling. Learning to associate the kinaesthetic handwriting movement with the visual letter pattern and the aural phonemes will help children with learning to spell.

While the traditional skills of handwriting still need to be taught, these skills now have to be delivered within a new curriculum.

Handwriting lessons can link effectively with early phonic and spelling work that will be happening in the classroom in the same term. *Penpals* fully exploits these overlap opportunities.

A practical approach

Penpals offers a practical approach to aid the delivery of handwriting teaching in the context of the modern curriculum:

- **Time** *Penpals'* focus on whole-class teaching, with key teaching points clearly identified, allows effective teaching in the time available.
- **Planning** *Penpals* helps with long-, medium- and short-term planning for each key stage, correlated to national guidelines.
- **Practice** *Penpals* offers pupil Practice Books with their own internal structure of excellent models for finger tracing and independent writing.
- **Revision** *Penpals* offers opportunities for record-keeping, review and assessment throughout the course.
- **Motivation** The *Penpals* materials are attractive and well designed with the support of handwriting experts to stimulate and motivate children.
- **ICT** Use the *Penpals* CD-ROMs to enrich and extend children's handwriting experiences.

A few words from the experts...

Professor Rhona Stainthorp *Professor, Institute of Education, University of Reading*

We now know that if children are to achieve comfortable, legible, flexible handwriting styles they need to be taught to form and join each letter efficiently. *Penpals* sets out to achieve this. Children need good models to copy, lots of practice and feedback to help them fine-tune their performance. This is accepted pedagogy in sport and music and we now know that it is also essential if children are to learn to write with legibility and speed. Legibility is important in order to communicate to others and to read one's own texts. Speed is essential so that the translation of thoughts into texts is not held back by the production of the letters.

If the practice element of letter formation includes the practice of spelling patterns, as in *Penpals*, the resultant pedagogy addresses two of the essential sub-skills of good written communication, namely handwriting and spelling.

Efficient handwriting leads to higher-quality writing.

Dr Rosemary Sassoon *Handwriting expert*

The Sassoon family of typefaces has been used throughout this scheme. Many people might therefore describe them as the model but they are typefaces, not exactly a handwriting model. No hand could copy them exactly and be so consistent and invariable. Equally, no typeface, however many alternative letters and joins are built in to a font, can be quite as flexible as handwritten letters. Our letters represent the movement, proportions and clear characteristics of basic separate and joined letters. It is likely that every teacher will produce his or her own slightly different version on the whiteboard, and pupils will then do likewise. It matters little if the slant or proportions of a child's writing differ slightly from any model. We are not teaching children to be forgers. We are equipping them with an efficient, legible handwriting that will serve them all their life – one that suits their hand and their personality. Flexibility is stressed throughout this scheme.

Links to national guidelines

Penpals Year 2/Primary 3 supports many National Guidelines including:

- *The National Curriculum for England and Wales*;
- *Primary Framework for literacy and mathematics* (Primary National Strategy 2006);
- *Letters and sounds – Principles and Practice of High Quality Phonics* (DfES 2007);
- *English Language 5–14 Guidelines* (The Scottish Office Education Department);
- *The Northern Ireland Curriculum: Primary* (CCEA).

Penpals and phonics

Penpals gives children the opportunity to revisit and consolidate their growing knowledge of phonics and spelling while securing the kinaesthetic movements needed for a legible, fast and fluent handwriting style.

In the *Penpals* Foundation 2, Year 1 and Year 2 CD-ROMs the word banks give opportunities for learning handwriting in the context of words that are easy to read and spell. After each handwriting movement has been introduced and practised it is recommended you revise the movement with a clear phonics focus in line with the appropriate *Letters and sounds* phase.

By Year 3 the transition from phonics into spelling has been made. All of the screens in the *Penpals* Year 3, Year 4 and Years 5 & 6 CD-ROMs create opportunities to revisit and secure spelling patterns while developing a confident and fluent handwriting style.

The chart links the units in the *Penpals* Year 2 CD-ROM with additional phonics practice. Also included in this chart are some high-frequency words that will be useful for practising spelling and for developing handwriting.

Year	Letters and sounds phase	Penpals Year 2 CD-ROM unit	Phonic words including high-frequency decodable words	High-frequency tricky and decodable words for additional practice
Year 2	6	3–5 *all diagonal joins*	beg/an, these, need, many, saw, them, see, had, dinosaur	because, said, called, asked, their, they, and, had, laug/hed, little
		6–10 *all horizontal joins*	good, told, house, down, for, bother, clothes, flower, bowling, whir/lpool	oh, what, ab/out, out, when, through, peop/le, could, looked, went
		11–15 *joining to and from r*	children, over, where, ran, your, very, carrot, girlf/riend, art, birthday	here, were, their, there, where, water, every/one, early, hard, bef/ore
		16–20 *joining to and from s*	fast, house, ask/ed, yesterday, washed, treasure, sunniest, cheese, Christmas, listen	should, Mrs, so, some, just, saw, said, she, was, these
		22–23 *joining to and from f*	fasten, swift, herself, fossil, flowering, few, prefix, reflection, leafy, fig/hting,	from, my/self, for, friends, fast, after, fish, first
		25–27 *joins rr, ss and ff*	session, missed, crossroads, hap/piness, carelessness, stiffest, buffet, different, g/iraffe, hurried	across, arrive, carry, horrib/le, tomorrow, address, class, cross, stiff, staffroom

Note: Underlining is used to show joins.

Classroom organisation

The ideal classroom organisation for teaching *Penpals* is to have the children sitting at desks or tables arranged so that they can all see the interactive white board (IWB). Each child needs a dry-wipe board (preferably with guidelines) and a marker pen or pencil and paper.

If this organisation is not possible within your classroom, bear in mind the following points as you plan your own classroom:

- All the children need to see the IWB and be able to copy words or handwriting patterns from it.
- Handwriting is usually done on a horizontal or slightly sloped surface.

When to use *Penpals*

Penpals can be used flexibly to teach handwriting. Ideally the whole-class teaching session will be followed immediately by the independent work, but where this is not possible the sessions may be split.

Timing the sessions

The whole-class session for each unit, including the warm-up activities, should take no more than 15 minutes. The independent working session should take about 15–20 minutes.

In addition to the allocated time, extra daily 'practice times' of 5–10 minutes are ideal.

Sequence for teaching the units

Gross and fine motor skills

The progression of the Foundation and Key Stage 1 lessons is generally assumed to be that of moving from gross to fine motor skills.

Teaching units

In Y2/P3 of *Penpals*, 10 units have been provided for the first two school terms. Term 3 has eight units with two extra assessment units. The units have been organised into a specific teaching sequence to ensure that skills are developed, practised and consolidated and that relevant phonic and spelling practice can be used.

Teaching sequence for a unit of *Penpals for Handwriting*

You will need:

- the Year 2 CD-ROM;
- the relevant Teacher's Book page;
- the Big Book or water-based marker pens for annotating the pages.

Children will need:

- space for both gross and fine motor skill warm ups;
- dry-wipe boards and marker pens;*
- pencils and coloured pencils;
- the Practice Book;
- handwriting exercise book.

(*Remember that one of the crucial elements of ensuring good handwriting is good posture. If children are writing with dry-wipe boards on their knees or on the floor, good posture is more difficult to achieve.)

Whole-class session

1 Warm up These ideas complement the gross and fine motor control warm-up clips accessible from the main menu of the CD-ROM. Use these at the start of the lesson to prepare the upper part of the body and the hands for handwriting.

2 Unit focus and phonic/spelling link These are clearly identified at the start of each unit.

4 Letter/join animations These provide opportunities to demonstrate and talk about correct letter/join formation. Children can practise tracing and copying the letters/joins.

5 Artwork These pictures represent a word relating to the focus join. Children identify the word and the relationship.

3 Units Every unit begins with a whole-class teaching session based on the CD-ROM.

6 Word bank These activities provide banks of differentiated words that you can use to model and discuss letter/join formation. Children can practise tracing the target letter/joins in words.

7 Group work Guidance for using the Big Book page with small groups to reinforce modelling the focus letters/joins in the context of longer texts.

9 Independent work See page 7.

8 Common errors Joining issues to look out for while children are working.

Independent work

This session can follow on directly from the whole-class session. Alternatively, it can be completed in other literacy time. Ideally, the children's work should be overseen by an adult to ensure correct formation and joining. The teacher's page for the unit provides helpful advice on using the Practice Book page together and highlights common errors to look out for.

At Key Stage 1 and Key Stage 2, children will need a handwriting exercise book to record their work in. They should have a sharpened pencil for their writing, but may also need coloured pencils for pattern practice.

The Practice Book pages offer:

1 Independent writing Practice of the focus join or joins.

2 Copying joins in context Once the children have practised writing the joins, they should try to write them in a context (usually a simple phrase or sentence, joke or rhyme).

3 High-frequency words Look, Say, Cover, Write, Check practice is provided for high-frequency words that feature the unit focus join (where possible).

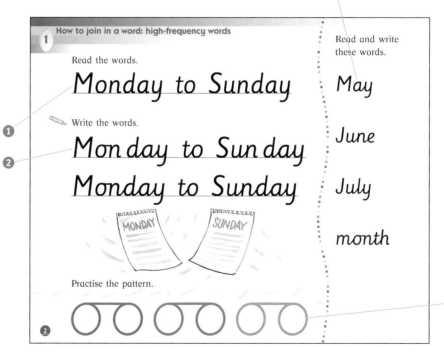

Also in the Teacher's Book:

Take aways These are photocopy masters (PCMs) for extra practice or homework. In addition to a PCM consolidating the unit focus, Units 3–28 direct you back to a PCM in Y1 for additional joining practice for children who need reinforcement.

4 Pattern practice Children will need to practise the patterns at the bottom of the page. These usually reflect the pencil movement of the unit focus, but always enhance fine motor control. These patterns can be made using coloured pencils. The patterns are artwork, not letters, and should be treated as opportunities to develop movement and control.

Differentiation

Differentiation using *Penpals* can be achieved in a number of ways:

- Children working individually with a Teaching Assistant may benefit from additional practice on dry-wipe boards.
- Take away activities provide excellent opportunities for differentiation as detailed above. Cross-references to similar Take aways in earlier books can help you to select less challenging activities for those who need extra practice at a lower level.
- Higher-achieving children can be challenged by higher expectations of control and evenness of letters. They may also be able to transfer more joins between sessions.

Assessment and record-keeping

On-going formative assessment

The most effective assessment of handwriting is on-going assessment because this gives you the chance to spot any errors or inconsistencies that are likely to impede a fast, fluent hand in the future. Be especially aware of left-handers and the difference between a pencil hold that will seriously limit their success in the future and one that has been found to work efficiently.

At Key Stage 1, a starting point assessment PCM is provided for use at the beginning of each school year (see page 9). This assesses the previous year's work and gives an indication of what needs to be consolidated before beginning new work.

On the teacher's page for every unit, the Common errors section draws attention to the most common mistakes children make.

The Practice Book page annotations in the Teacher's Book also enable you to draw the children's attention to particular handwriting issues.

Summative assessment

Beginning of year

The PCM on page 9 can be used for an assessment to ensure that all children are ready for *Penpals: Y2/P3*. If children's letter formation is still insecure, they will benefit from revising units in *Penpals: Y1/P2*.

End of year

From Y1/P2 you can use text from the final unit in each book as the basis of a summative assessment. (Units 29 and 30 in the books for Years 2–4 may be particularly helpful as SATs practice.) As you do the summative assessment, consider key handwriting issues:

- Are all letters formed correctly?
- Are letters consistently sized?
- Are known joins used?
- Are they used correctly?
- Are ascenders and descenders parallel?
- Are spaces within and between words regular?
- Is good handwriting carried over into cross-curricular activities?
- What are the next handwriting targets for this child?

Record-keeping

- The best record of what children have achieved will be in their handwriting books. It is therefore important to keep a book specifically for this purpose. This will provide a useful record of achievement to share with parents and colleagues.
- The Contents page can be photocopied and used with highlighting pens and dates to keep a record of which units have been completed. You may find it helpful to use a 'traffic light' system (green highlighter pen for 'achieved', yellow for 'not totally secure' and pink for 'not achieved') to highlight units you need to revisit with individuals, groups or the whole class.

Children's beginning of year assessment

Name .... Date ....

Write the alphabet in lower case letters (*a, b, c, d, e, ...*).

_____

_____

Write the alphabet in capital letters (A, B, C, D, E, ...).

_____

_____

Copy these joins	and these words.	Copy these joins	and these words.
lp	help	fr	frog
ck	duck	ot	hot
nd	hand	wh	when
ng	sing	oo	look
wi	with		

Glossary of key terms

Talking about handwriting

Throughout *Penpals* it has been assumed that correct terminology should be used as soon as possible. At Key Stage 1 there is an emphasis on talking about letter formation in the context of joining.

Terms used in *Penpals* include:

- **Lower case letter.**
- **Capital letter** is used in preference to 'upper case letter'.
- **Short letter** is the term used to describe a letter with no ascender or descender.
- **Letter with an ascender, letter with a descender.**
- **Flick** is used to describe an exit stroke (note that t finishes with a curl to the right rather than merely an exit flick).
- **Curve** is used to describe the descender on letters (y, j, g, f).
- **Cross bar** is used to describe the left-to-right line on t and f. It may also be used in relation to letters that feature a left-to-right horizontal line (e.g. e and z).
- **Diagonal join to ascender** (e.g. at), **diagonal join (no ascender)** (e.g. du), **diagonal join to an anticlockwise letter** (e.g. ho).
- **Horizontal join to ascender** (e.g. oh), **horizontal join (no ascender)** (e.g. re), **horizontal join to an anticlockwise letter** (e.g. wo).
- **Break letters** are letters from which no join has yet been taught. (See notes on formation of specific letters and joins.)
- Other important terminology used throughout *Penpals* includes **vertical, parallel, joined, sloped, anticlockwise**.

Key CD-ROM features

- **Warm-up clips** These activities may be linked to the focus of the unit but are generally just enjoyable movement activities to warm up the muscles.
- **Letter/join animations** These animations encourage the children to watch and sky write as the focus letter/join animates on the screen.
- **Word bank** This provides a useful bank of words that enable you to demonstrate the focus letters/joins.
- **Show alphabet** These animations show how to form all capital and lower case letters.

Notes on formation of specific letters and joins

Correct letter formation can be demonstrated using the **Show alphabet** section on the CD-ROM.

- k – the use of the curly form of k, as opposed to the straight k is recommended by handwriting experts because its flowing form lends itself more naturally to joining. It is also more easily distinguished from the capital letter.
- o – there is no exit stroke from the lower case o when it is not joined. Unlike the flick at the bottom of letters like n and l, the exit stroke from the o is not an integral part of the letter, but simply a mechanism for joining.
- e – two different forms of e (e/e) are used in order to show children how it alters when other letters are joined to it.
- f, q, r, s – letters that the children are taught to join in Y2/P3.
- b and p – letters that the children are taught to join in Y3/P4.
- g, j, y – letters that are not joined from, though there is some exploration of joining them in Y5&6/P6&7.
- x and z are never joined to or from as these are uncomfortable joins that often result in the malformation of both the joining letter and the x or z. Also, handwriting is generally faster and more legible if it is not continuously joined.

Capital letters

Capitals are taught in the Foundation 2 materials and then revisited in subsequent years as appropriate. It is generally agreed that there is no right or wrong way to form capitals. However, there is a general principle of forming them from top to bottom and left to right wherever possible. Consideration should also be given to whether a letter formation will deteriorate when written at speed. As skills and confidence develop, left-handers may well form capitals differently (they have a tendency to go from right to left, for example). This should not be an issue as capitals are never joined.

- **Capital** Y – the use of a central stalk (as opposed to a slanting stalk) is recommended as, once children have completed the 'v' form at the top of the letter, they have a clear starting point for the downwards stroke. This formation also distinguishes the capital letter from the lower case letter and retains its shape when written at speed.
- **Capital** G – this form of G is recommended as the correct handwriting form of the letter. Variations which include a vertical line (G) are font forms.
- **Capital** H – the formation of H using two down strokes followed by the horizontal stroke from left to right is recommended. The alternative (one down stroke followed by a horizontal and a further down stroke) can quickly resemble the letter M when written at speed.
- **Capital** K – this formation of K (with two pencil strokes rather than three) is recommended as it is more fluently formed when writing at speed.

In order to promote fluent handwriting and to support the early stages of spelling, some handwriting joins are introduced in Y1/P2 as soon as all individual letter formation is secure.

Throughout the Key Stage 1 resources, new joins are introduced in a unit that presents a variety of words featuring those joins. In Y2/P3, children are given opportunities to practise joins that they have already learnt. Children are never expected to copy text featuring joins that they have not been formally taught.

Progression in the introduction of joins

Y1/P2 In these resources only two or three letters in a word are joined. The words on the CD-ROM and in the Big Book and the Practice Book feature the focus join for the teaching unit.

Y2/P3 As more joins are introduced, children are given opportunities to practise familiar joins which are not the focus of the unit. During the year, children are expected to begin to join all the letters in a short word, or to join letter patterns which can support spelling choices.

If children in Y2/P3 have not been introduced to joining before, it should be noted that the first ten units of Y2/P3 revise all the basic joins. Additionally we suggest that, rather than immediately joining whole words, words are 'chunked', as demonstrated. Some children may also benefit from working on Y1/P2 PCMs for further consolidation.

The sequence for *Penpals*: Y2/P3 is:

Term 1   Revising familiar joins – no new joins.
New: combining joins in a word leading to whole words.

Term 2   Revising joins in a word.
New: joining from *r* and to and from *s*.

Term 3   Revising joins in a word, revising capital letters.
New: joining from *f*, joining *ff*, *ss*, *rr*, *qu*.
Assessment.

Y3&4/P4&5 All the basic joins will now be familiar. In these resources, children are asked to practise 'tricky joins' and to begin to develop fluent, even handwriting. An emphasis on spacing between letters and words, consistency of letter size, parallel ascenders and descenders helps children to present their work well.

Y4/P5 Children are introduced to a sloped style of writing and are expected to write mostly in pen.

Y5&6/P6&7 Two sets of OHTs are provided for each of these year groups, one with a handwriting focus, the other with a project focus.

Defining the joins

(See the inside back cover of this Teacher's Book for a list of letter sets requiring each of the joins as taught in Y2/P3.)

The two basic join types

- **Diagonal join** (introduced in Y1/P2, Unit 11): this is the most common join. It starts from the final flick on the baseline (or 'curl' in the case of the letter *t*). Letters which come before a diagonal join are: *a*, *b*, *c*, *d*, *e*, *h*, *i*, *k*, *l*, *m*, *n*, *p*, *s*, *t*, *u* (and *q*, in which the flick begins below the baseline).
- **Horizontal join** (introduced in Y1/P2, Unit 24): this join is formed from letters which finish at the top of the letter rather than at the baseline. Letters which come before a horizontal join are: *f*, *o*, *r*, *v*, *w*.

Variations on the join types

Penpals uses three subsets of the main joins: join to a letter with an ascender, join to a letter with no ascender and join to a letter that begins with an anticlockwise movement. Since the last subset involves stopping the pencil and reversing the direction of movement, these are called *diagonal join to an anticlockwise letter* and *horizontal join to an anticlockwise letter*. Joins to anticlockwise letters are trickier to teach and need more practice than straightforward diagonal and horizontal joins. These joins tend to 'decay' when children begin to write more quickly.

- **Diagonal join to a letter with an ascender** (e.g. *ub*) (introduced in Y1/P2, Unit 11): this is a variation of the diagonal join.
- **Diagonal join to an anticlockwise letter** (e.g. *ho*) (introduced in Y1/P2, Unit 18): joining with a diagonal join to the anticlockwise letters in the 'curly caterpillar' family involves stopping the hand movement and reversing it. This can be a tricky join and it decays easily in fast writing.
- **Horizontal join to an anticlockwise letter** (e.g. *wo*) (introduced in Y1/P2, Unit 26): joining from a horizontal join to an anticlockwise letter involves a reversal.
- **Horizontal join to a letter with an ascender** (e.g. *oh*) (introduced in Y1/P2, Unit 28): this is a slightly sloped version of a horizontal join.
- **Break letters** (introduced in Y2/P3): these are letters from which no join has yet been taught. (See notes on page 10.)

Join patter for *Penpals*

This chart shows the oral patter for the formation of joins.

Diagonal join to ascender: *at, all*	Slope all the way up from the flick to begin the next letter.
Diagonal join, no ascender	Slope up from the flick to begin the next letter.
Diagonal join, no ascender, to an anticlockwise letter	Slope up from the flick and round to begin the curve.
Horizontal join, no ascender	Across from the top to begin the next letter.
Horizontal join, no ascender, to an anticlockwise letter	Across from the top and round to begin the curve.
Horizontal join to ascender	Across from the top and slope all the way up to begin the next letter.
Diagonal join to ascender, to an anticlockwise letter	Slope all the way up from the flick and round to begin the curve.
Horizontal join to ascender, to an anticlockwise letter	Across from the top and all the way up and round to begin the curve.
Break letters	Lift and start the next letter.
Horizontal join from *r* to ascender	Over and dip, and slope all the way up to begin the next letter.
Horizontal join from *r*	Over and dip to begin the next letter.
Diagonal join to *s*	Slope up from the flick and round to begin a 'small curve' *s*.
Horizontal join to *s*	Across from the top, dip and round to begin a 'small curve' *s*.
Diagonal join from *s* to ascender	Swing all the way up from the bottom curve to begin the next letter.
Diagonal join from *s*, no ascender	Swing up from the bottom curve to begin the next letter.
Horizontal join from *r* to an anticlockwise letter	Over and dip, and round to begin the curve.
Horizontal join (to and) from *f* to ascender	Across the bar and slope all the way up to begin the next letter.
Horizontal join from *f*, no ascender	Across the bar to begin the next letter.
qu	Slope up from the flick to begin the *u*.
rr	Over and dip to begin the next letter.
ss	Swing up from the bottom curve to begin a 'small curve' *s*.
ff	Across the bar and slope all the way up and round to begin the curve.
Joining *b* and *p*	Swing up from the bottom curve to begin the next letter.

Planning staff INSET

When you introduce *Penpals* into your school, it is important to ensure that all the staff in the school follow the scheme. Suggestions are given on page 11 to support the introduction of the programme throughout the school as there may be issues for children who have not met joining before. It may be useful to hold an INSET staff meeting. The following pages in this book are photocopiable to make OHTs for this purpose:

- page 14 – outline of INSET session;
- page 15 – information sheet for parents;
- page 16 – variations of the font;
- pages 62 and 63 – handwriting mats;
- page 64 – photocopiable ruled sheet for handwriting practice;
- inside back cover – joining letter sets (also appears on the inside front cover of the Big Book and Practice Book).

Suggested topics for inclusion in INSET meeting

Organisational issues

- **Rationale for introducing *Penpals for Handwriting*** Use the information on page 4.
- **Classroom organisation** Copy page 5 of this introduction for all staff. Read through it together, agreeing on the most appropriate time for the sessions, etc.
- **Assessment and record-keeping** Use the information on page 8.
- **Home–school links** Make an OHT of the information sheet on page 14.

Handwriting issues

- **Font** Use the **Show alphabet** section on the CD-ROM to demonstrate the font. Information on page 10 of the introduction may be used to clarify any issues arising.
- **Font size** Photocopy page 16 of this Teacher's Book to demonstrate how font size is shown throughout *Penpals*.
- **Joins and break letters** Use the **Show joining letter sets** section on the CD-ROM, or an OHT of the inside back cover of this book, to demonstrate the joining letter sets and the break letters.
- **Writing on lined paper** Children should be encouraged to write on lined paper from the time they begin to focus on correct letter formation and orientation. As the children's handwriting becomes more controlled, the width between the lines should decrease. It may well be that at any given time different children in your class will benefit from writing on paper with different line widths. The size of the font in the Practice Books is intended to reflect a development in handwriting. However, you should still tailor the handwriting materials to meet the needs of individual children in your class. A photocopiable sheet with lines of a suitable width is provided on page 64. (If any children require a narrower rule, use the photocopiable sheet from page 64 of the Y3/P4 Teacher's Book.) Some children may prefer to write on lined paper which also includes guidelines for the height of ascenders and descenders.
- **Pencil hold** Use the pencil hold videos in the **Posture clips** section on the CD-ROM to illustrate good pencil hold. The traditionally recommended pencil hold allows children to sustain handwriting for long periods without tiring their hands. However, there are many alternative pencil holds (particularly for left-handers) and the most important thing is comfort and a hold that will be efficient under speed. Some children may benefit from triangular pencils or ordinary pencils with plastic pencil grips.

- **Posture** Use the photographs in the **Posture clips** section on the CD-ROM to illustrate good posture. A good posture and pencil hold are vital for good handwriting. Although many young children enjoy sitting on one foot, kneeling or wrapping their feet around the legs of the chair, they will find it easier to sustain good handwriting comfortably if they adopt a good posture.
- **Left-handed children** Left-handed children should not sit to the right of right-handed children as their papers will meet in the middle! Left-handed children should be taught to position their paper to the left of centre and then angle the paper for comfort as suggested below. Use the left-handed pencil hold video and posture photograph in the **Posture clips** section on the CD-ROM to illustrate this. There is no reason why left-handed children's handwriting should be any worse than that of right-handed children.
- **Sloped surfaces** Children who experience some motor control difficulties often benefit from writing on a slight slope. The easiest and cheapest way to provide this in the classroom is to use substantial A4 or foolscap ring-binders of which there are usually plenty in school. Commercial wooden or plastic writing slopes are also widely available.
- **Angle of paper** Make an OHT of the guidelines for right- and left-handed children as provided on pages 62 and 63. You can photocopy these onto A3 paper and laminate them to make table-top mats for the children. Use the spaces provided to allow children to find the optimum position. Show the children how to line up the corners of their books to create a comfortable angle for writing, or how to use Blu-Tack to secure their paper to the mats to produce guidelines when writing on blank paper. These guidelines provide a good guide but encourage the children to explore personal variation of the angles.

Organisational issues

- ## Rationale
  - a flexible, fluent and legible handwriting style
  - a 5-stage developmental process
  - active teaching in association with phonics and spelling

- ## Classroom organisation
  - weekly teaching sessions with little-and-often practice

- ## Assessment and record-keeping
  - beginning of year assessment for each year
  - group encourages self assessment

- ## Home-school links
  - parent information sheets for each year
  - homework activities

Handwriting issues
font, font size, joins and break letters, writing on lined paper, pencil hold, posture, left-handed children, sloped surfaces, angle of paper

Penpals for Handwriting: Year 2 information sheet for parents

The main aim during this year is for children to begin to develop an easy and clear handwriting style which can become fluent and automatic. This will help to prepare children for writing and spelling tasks during the school year.

Letter formation of capitals and lower case letters should now be familiar and secure.

Children have been introduced to the two basic join types:
- Joins from the baseline, known as **diagonal joins**, including:
  - diagonal join, no ascender, e.g. *am, un, lp*
  - diagonal join to an ascender, e.g. *at, th, ck*
  - diagonal join to an anti-clockwise letter, e.g. *ag, nd, if*
- Joins from the crossbar, known as **horizontal joins**, including:
  - horizontal join, no ascender, e.g. *op, wi*
  - horizontal join to an ascender, e.g. *ot, wh*
  - horizontal join to an anticlockwise letter, e.g. *oo, wa*

Break letters (i.e. letters which are not joined from at this stage) include: *b, g, j, p, y, x, z.*

New joining letters introduced during this year are:
- Join from q: e.g. *quick, quiet, queen*
- Joins to and from r: e.g. *ran, her, hurry*
- Joins to and from s: e.g. *has, sent, class*
- Joins from f: e.g. *far, fluffy*

So far, children have only tried joining one pair of letters in a word. This year they will gradually learn to join more letters in a word, using all the different joins: e.g. *calculator, kitten, handwriting.*

To begin with, however, children will focus on joining letters that combine to make a common letter pattern (e.g. *ee* as in *feet*; *oi* as in *foil*; *oa* as in *boat*). Learning to combine letters in this way links handwriting with spelling and helps children to become more confident spellers.

Variations in font throughout *Penpals*

FIVE DEVELOPMENTAL PHASES	SASSOON® CAMBRIDGE JOINER	*Penpals* Progression	*Penpals* typesizes*
1 GROSS AND FINE MOTOR SKILLS AND LETTER FORMATION		Each letter family is introduced with finger tracing letters incorporating the letter family artwork and a starting dot.	***a*** **Foundation 2/Primary 1** 21mm/11.5mm
		Hollow letters with starting dots and arrows to show correct letter formation are also used for finger tracing.	***a*** **Year 1/Primary 2** 17mm/8mm
	c	Solid letters with starting dots support letter formation.	*a* **Year 2/Primary 3** 5.5mm
	d	Independent writing with exit flicks is encouraged in preparation for joining.	*a* **Year 3/Primary 4** 4mm
2 BEGINNING TO JOIN	*pen*	Red is used for the focus join and joining letters to teach fluent letter formation.	*a* **Year 4 onwards/ Primary 5 onwards** sloped, 4mm
3 SECURING THE JOINS	*secure*	Once all joins have been taught, all words are shown as joined for practice and consolidation.	
4 PRACTISING SPEED AND FLUENCY	*faster*	Children are encouraged to develop an individual style for speed and legibility.	
5 PRESENTATION SKILLS	*individual* **print** *jokey*	Further development of an individual style as well as presentation skills and techniques.	

* Letters in red are for finger tracing. Letters in black are writing models.

1 How to join in a word: high-frequency words

Warm up

👋 Children reach up high and bend down low.
👋 Children name the days of the week and count them on their fingers.

CD-ROM

Unit focus: beginning to link joins within words.
Phonics and spelling link: high-frequency words.

Artwork
The picture illustrates a word from the word bank. Children identify the word and establish the patterns for chunking.

Join animations
Focus on different choices for joining. Emphasise that sometimes joining can be used to support spelling.

Word bank
Choose a word to discuss. Click on the word to make it grey for exploring ways of joining. Model and discuss the different ways of joining within the word.

Group work

Introduce the page
● Ask the children to look at the words on the page. Explain that you're going to learn how to join up more than two letters within words. This will help them write more easily and quickly.

Demonstrate the join
● Prepare the Big Book page by covering all but the top line of each box with Post-it notes.
● Look at the word *when*. Tell children that you can break the word down into chunks (which you can then join together).
  Get Up and Go Ask the children to come up and point to the chunks that they already know how to join.
● Reveal the second line and trace over the *wh* and the *en*.
● Explain that you can now join these chunks together, then trace over the whole word *when*, emphasising the smooth and flowing movement of your hand.
● Repeat the process for *then* and *with*.
  Show Me Children practise 'chunking' the word *that* and then writing it fully joined.
● Model how to chunk and join *that* in the spaces provided.

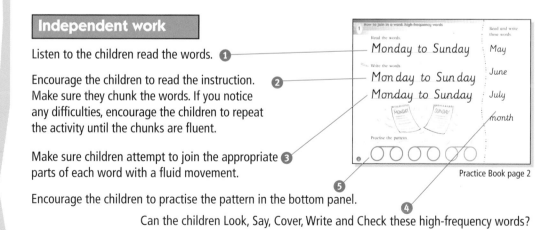

Big Book page 2

Independent work

Listen to the children read the words. **1**

Encourage the children to read the instruction. **2** Make sure they chunk the words. If you notice any difficulties, encourage the children to repeat the activity until the chunks are fluent.

Make sure children attempt to join the appropriate **3** parts of each word with a fluid movement.

Encourage the children to practise the pattern in the bottom panel. **5**

4

Can the children Look, Say, Cover, Write and Check these high-frequency words?

Practice Book page 2

Common errors
● writing chunks of words at incorrect relative heights *When*
● children hesitating after each chunk, not making the word fluent

Take away

For additional practice of joining high-frequency words use **PCM 1**.

2 Introducing the break letters: *j, g, x, y, z, b, f, p, q, r, s*

Warm up

🖐 Children make their whole bodies wobble like a jelly.

🖐 Children make their hands wobble like a jelly.

Unit focus: introducing break letters (including tricky joins *b, f, p, q, r, s,* that will be taught later).

Phonics and spelling links: reinforcing initial consonant work from Y1/P2; practising handwriting patterns from Y1/P2.

Artwork

The picture illustrates words from the word bank. Children identify the words (e.g. zany, fluffy, quacking). Write the words and establish any break letters.

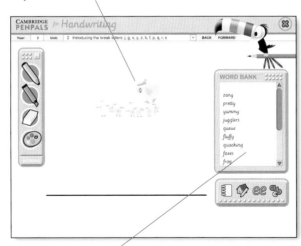

Word bank

Choose a word to practise writing with break letters. Click on the word to make it grey. Children can continue to chunk the other letters to support spelling.

Group work

Introduce the page

● Ask the children to look at the letters in the box and to read the phrases.

Demonstrate the join

● Explain that the letters on the top line of the box are special ones that you don't join from. Tell children that, at the moment, they don't have to join from the letters on the bottom line either, but that they'll be learning to join these letters a bit later on. Joining to *s* is a special teaching point in later units.

● Model tracing over the phrases, emphasising the points at which you break rather than join.

Show Me Children practise writing the phrases.

Independent work

Watch the children write the letters. ❶

Encourage the children to read the ❷ instruction and write the words. Make sure they join and break in the appropriate places.

Practice Book page 3

Encourage the children to practise the pattern in the bottom panel. ❸

Can the children Look, Say, Cover, Write and Check these high-frequency words?

Take away

For additional practice of the break letters use **PCM 2**.

Common errors

● trying to join the break letters at this stage

3 Practising diagonal join to ascender in words: *eel*, *eet*

*Three wheels
with teeth!*

Big Book page 4

Warm up

✋ Children imitate the motion of train wheels with their arms, moving them backwards and forwards.

✋ Children make snapping mouths with their hands, using straight and then bent fingers.

CD-ROM

Unit focus: joining *eel*, *eet*.

Phonics and spelling link: reinforcing long vowel phoneme **ee**.

Artwork

The picture illustrates a word from the word bank. Children identify the word and find the target letter pattern.

Join animations

The letter patterns demonstrate the diagonal join to ascender. Reinforce the flowing movement in this familiar join. Check that letter height and appropriate spacing are maintained.

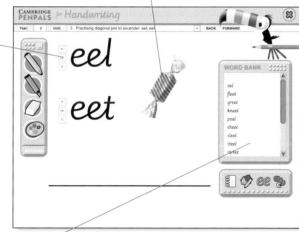

Word bank

Choose a word to practise diagonal joins to ascender. Click on the word to make the focus join grey. Children should be able to join all the letters in these words, with the exception of the break letters.

Common errors

- incorrect joining of *ee*, misshaping the *e* *eet*
- horizontal rather than diagonal join from the *e* to the ascender

Group work

NB: *s* is not joined to at this stage; joins to *s* will be dealt with later.

Introduce the page

- Ask the children to look at the picture and read the words on the page.
- Talk about the formation of an exclamation mark.

Demonstrate the join

Get Up and Go Cover the writing in grey and ask the children to come up and show you which letters can be joined in each word. Remind the children that capital letters never join. Can anyone spot the other letters that don't join? (*r* in *three* and *s* in *wheels*)

- If you wish, you can go through an intermediate stage, where you chunk the words before joining them completely.
- Model tracing over the joined words in grey, emphasising the smooth and flowing movement of your hand.

Show Me Children practise writing the joined words. (They can practise chunking the words first if that is more appropriate.)

Independent work

Encourage the children to read the instruction. ❶ Make sure they chunk the words. If you notice any difficulties, encourage the children to repeat the activity until the chunks are fluent.

Listen to the children read the sentence. ❷ Ask them to spot which letters aren't joined. Make sure they attempt to join the appropriate parts of each word with a fluid movement.

Encourage the children to practise the pattern in the bottom panel.

Can the children Look, Say, Cover, Write and Check these words?

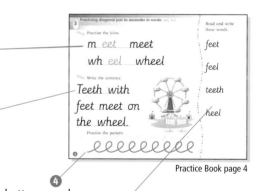

Practice Book page 4

Take away

① For additional practice of these joins use **PCM 3**.

② For additional practice of this group of joins use **Year 1 PCMs 11–14** (introducing and practising diagonal join to ascender).

4 Practising diagonal join, no ascender, in words: *a_e*

Warm up

🖐 Children wave close to their bodies and far away, up high, to the left and to the right.

🖐 Children make each of their fingers wave.

CD-ROM

Unit focus: joining *a_e*.
Phonics and spelling link: reinforcing long vowel phoneme **ai**.

Artwork
The picture illustrates a word from the word bank. Children identify the word and find the target letter pattern.

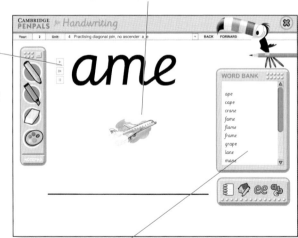

Join animation
The letter pattern demonstrates the diagonal join, no ascender. Reinforce the flowing movement in this familiar join. Check that letter height and appropriate spacing are maintained.

Word bank
Choose a word to practise diagonal joins, no ascender. Click on the word to make the focus join grey. Children should be able to join all the letters in these words, with the exception of the break letters.

Common errors
● joining the break letters

Group work

Introduce the page

● Ask the children to look at the picture and read the words on the page.

● Talk about the speech marks, apostrophe and comma.

Demonstrate the join

Get Up and Go Cover the writing in grey and ask the children to come up and show you which letters can be joined in each word. Remind the children that capital letters never join. Can anyone spot the other letters that don't join? (*p* in *play* and *g* in *game* and *s* in *same*)

● If you wish, you can go through an intermediate stage, where you chunk the words before joining them completely.

● Model tracing over the joined words in grey, emphasising the smooth and flowing movement of your hand.

Show Me Children practise writing the joined words. (They can practise chunking the words first if that is more appropriate.)

"Let's play the same game, Shane."

"Let's play the same game, Shane."

Let's race!

Big Book page 5

Independent work

Encourage the children to read the instruction. ❶ Make sure they chunk the words. If you notice any difficulties, encourage the children to repeat the activity until the chunks are fluent.

Listen to the children read the sentence. ❷ Ask them to spot which letters aren't joined. Make sure they attempt to join the appropriate parts of each word with a fluid movement.

Encourage the children to practise the pattern in the bottom panel. ❸ ❹

Can the children Look, Say, Cover, Write and Check these words?

c_age   cage   came
n_ame   name   made

Put a name plate   name
on Dane's cage.
*   game*

Practice Book page 5

Take away

① For additional practice of this join use **PCM 4**.

② For additional practice of this group of joins use **Year 1 PCMs 15–17** (introducing and practising diagonal join, no ascender).

5 Practising diagonal join, no ascender, to an anticlockwise letter in words: *ice*, *ide*

Warm up

- Children make swooshing slide movements with their arms.
- Children make mouse whiskers with their fingers.

CD-ROM

Unit focus: joining *ice*, *ide*.
Phonics and spelling link: reinforcing long vowel phoneme **ie**.

Artwork

The picture illustrates a word from the word bank. Children identify the word and find the target letter pattern.

Join animations

The letter patterns demonstrate the diagonal join, no ascender, to an anticlockwise letter. Reinforce the flowing movement in this familiar join. Check that letter height and appropriate spacing are maintained.

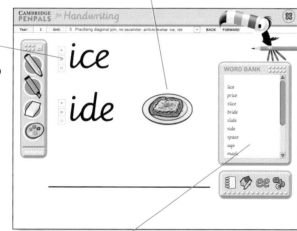

Word bank

Choose a word to practise diagonal joins, no ascender, to an anticlockwise letter. Click on the word to make the focus join grey. Children should be able to join all the letters in these words, with the exception of the break letters.

Common errors

- making the *d* of *ide* the same size as the *c* of *ice*   *ide*   *ice*
- dotting the *i* before the word is finished

Group work

NB: *s* is not joined to at this stage; joins to *s* will be dealt with later.

Introduce the page

- Ask the children to look at the pictures and read the letters on the page. Ask them what they think the *ice* machine is for.

Demonstrate the join

- Explain that you're going to use the *ice* machine and the *ide* slide to make some new words.
- Point to each letter in turn and ask children what word it will make when added to *ice*.
- Model tracing over the joined letters.
- Model writing the joined word in the space below.
  Show Me Children can try writing a joined word for themselves.
- Repeat with the *ide* slide.

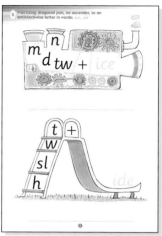

Big Book page 6

Independent work

Encourage the children to read the instruction. ❶
Make sure they chunk the words. If you notice any difficulties, encourage the children to repeat the activity until the chunks are fluent.

Listen to the children read the sentence. ❷
Ask them to spot which letters aren't joined.
Make sure they attempt to join the appropriate parts of each word with a fluid movement.

Encourage the children to practise the pattern in the bottom panel.

Can the children Look, Say, Cover, Write and Check these words?

Practice Book page 6

Take away

① For additional practice of this join use **PCM 5**.

② For additional practice of this group of joins use **Year 1 PCMs 18–20** (introducing and practising diagonal join, no ascender, to an anticlockwise letter).

6 Practising horizontal join, no ascender, in words: *ow*, *ou*

Warm up

- 🖐 Children make circles in the air with their arms.
- 🖐 Children trace circles round and round on the palms of their hands.

CD-ROM

Unit focus: joining *ow*, *ou*.
Phonics and spelling links: vowel phoneme **ow**; words with the same sounds but different spellings.

Artwork
The picture illustrates a word from the word bank. Children identify the word and find the target letter pattern.

Join animations
The letter patterns demonstrate the horizontal join, no ascender. Reinforce the flowing movement in this familiar join. Check that letter height and appropriate spacing are maintained.

Word bank
Choose a word to practise horizontal joins, no ascender. Click on the word to make the focus join grey. Children should be able to join all the letters in these words, with the exception of the break letters.

Common errors
- incorrect relative heights
- crossing the *o* and misdirecting the join

Group work

NB: *s* is not joined to at this stage; joins to *s* will be dealt with later.

Introduce the page
- Ask the children to look at the picture and read the words on the page. The sign offers an opportunity to discuss capitals.

Demonstrate the join
   Get Up and Go Cover the words in grey and ask the children to come up and show you which letters can be joined in each word. Remind the children that capital letters never join. Can anyone spot the other letter that doesn't join? (*s* in *house*)
- If you wish, you can go through an intermediate stage, where you chunk the words before joining them completely.
- Model tracing over the joined words in grey, emphasising the smooth and flowing movement of your hand.
   Show Me Children practise writing the joined words. (They can practise chunking the words first if that is more appropriate.)

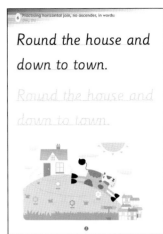

Round the house and down to town.

Big Book page 7

Independent work

Encourage the children to read the instruction. ❶
Make sure they chunk the words. If you notice any difficulties, encourage the children to repeat the activity until the chunks are fluent.

Listen to the children read the joke. ❷
Ask them to spot which letters aren't joined.
Make sure they attempt to join the appropriate parts of each word with a fluid movement.

Encourage the children to practise the pattern in the bottom panel. ❸

❹

Can the children Look, Say, Cover, Write and Check these high-frequency words?

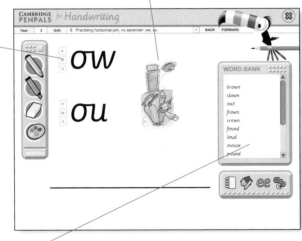

Practice Book page 7

Take away

① For additional practice of this join use **PCM 6**.

② For additional practice of this group of joins use **Year 1 PCMs 24 and 25** (introducing and practising horizontal join, no ascender).

Warm up

👆 Children make large spirals in the air with their arms.
👆 Children draw small spirals on the palm of each hand using their fingers.

CD-ROM

Unit focus: joining *oy, oi*.
Phonics and spelling links: vowel phoneme **oy**;
words with the same sounds but different spellings.

Artwork

The picture illustrates a word from the word bank. Children identify the word and find the target letter pattern.

Join animations

The letter patterns demonstrate the horizontal join, no ascender. Reinforce the flowing movement in this familiar join. Check that letter height and appropriate spacing are maintained.

Word bank

Choose a word to practise horizontal joins, no ascender. Click on the word to make the focus join grey. Children should be able to join all the letters in these words, with the exception of the break letters.

Common errors

● not closing the *o*, moving on to the join too quickly
● too short a descender on the *y*

Group work

Introduce the page

● Ask the children to look at the picture and read the words on the page.

Demonstrate the join

Get Up and Go Cover the words in grey and ask the children to come up and show you which letters can be joined in each word. Remind the children that capital letters never join. Can anyone spot the other letters that don't join? (*f* in *foil*, *b* in *boil* and *j* in *joy*)

● If you wish, you can go through an intermediate stage, where you chunk the words before joining them completely.

● Model tracing over the joined words in grey, emphasising the smooth and flowing movement of your hand.
Show Me Children practise writing the joined words. (They can practise chunking the words first if that is more appropriate.)

Coil in foil then boil with joy.

Big Book page 8

Independent work

Encourage the children to read the instruction. **1**
Make sure they chunk the words. If you notice any difficulties, encourage the children to repeat the activity until the chunks are fluent.

Listen to the children read the sentence. **2**
Ask them to spot which letters aren't joined.
Make sure they attempt to join the appropriate parts of each word with a fluid movement.

Encourage the children to practise the pattern in the bottom panel.

Can the children Look, Say, Cover, Write and Check these words?

Practice Book page 8

Take away

① For additional practice of this join use **PCM 7**.

② For additional practice of this group of joins use **Year 1 PCMs 24 and 25** (introducing and practising horizontal join, no ascender).

23

8 Practising horizontal join, no ascender, to an anticlockwise letter in words: *oa, ode*

Warm up

👋 Children link hands in front of them and stretch, then move arms above heads and stretch again.

👋 Children stretch their hands as wide as they can, then make fists.

CD-ROM

Unit focus: joining *oa, ode*.
Phonics and spelling link: reinforcing long vowel phoneme **oa**.

Artwork

The picture illustrates a word from the word bank. Children identify the word and find the target letter pattern.

Join animations

The letter patterns demonstrate the horizontal join, no ascender, to an anticlockwise letter. Reinforce the flowing movement in this familiar join. Check that letter height and appropriate spacing are maintained.

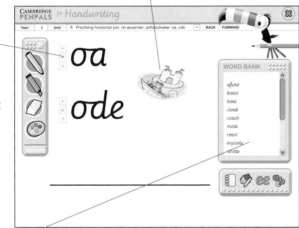

Word bank

Choose a word to practise horizontal joins, no ascender, to an anticlockwise letter. Click on the word to make the focus join grey. Children should be able to join all the letters in these words, with the exception of the break letters.

Common errors

● not reversing on the *a* or reversing too far
● crossing the *o* and joining at too steep an angle

Group work

Introduce the page

● Ask the children to look at the pictures and read the words on the page.

● Discuss the question mark.

Demonstrate the join

Get Up and Go Cover the words in grey and ask the children to come up and show you which letters can be joined in each word. Remind the children that capital letters never join. Can anyone spot the other letters that don't join? (*s* in *toast* and *f* in *float*)

● If you wish, you can go through an intermediate stage, where you chunk the words before joining them completely.

● Model tracing over the joined words at the bottom of the page, emphasising the smooth and flowing movement of your hand.
Show Me Children practise writing the joined words. (They can practise chunking the words first if that is more appropriate.)

● Ask the children to answer the question by putting a tick or a cross in each box.

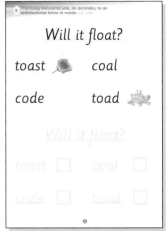

Will it float?

toast   coal

code   toad

Big Book page 9

Independent work

Encourage the children to read the instruction. **1**
Make sure they chunk the words. If you notice any difficulties, encourage the children to repeat the activity until the chunks are fluent.

Listen to the children read the sentence. **2**
Ask them to spot which letters aren't joined. Make sure they attempt to join the appropriate parts of each word with a fluid movement.

Encourage the children to practise the pattern in the bottom panel.

Can the children Look, Say, Cover, Write and Check these words?

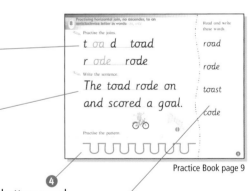

Practice Book page 9

Take away

① For additional practice of this join use **PCM 8**.

② For additional practice of this group of joins use **Year 1 PCMs 26 and 27** (introducing and practising horizontal join, no ascender, to an anticlockwise letter).

9 Practising horizontal join to ascender in words: *ole, obe*

Warm up

✋ Children make a large loop by putting their arms above their heads and linking their fingers. They move it down in front of them to shoulder height, then turn to the left and the right, taking their loop with them.

✋ Children make small loops with their thumb and each finger in turn. Repeat with the opposite hand.

CD-ROM

Unit focus: joining *ole, obe*.

Phonics and spelling link: reinforcing long vowel phoneme **oa**.

Artwork

The picture illustrates a word from the word bank. Children identify the word and find the target letter pattern.

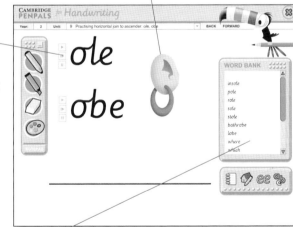

Join animations

The letter patterns demonstrate the horizontal join to ascender. Reinforce the flowing movement in this familiar join. Check that letter height and appropriate spacing are maintained.

Word bank

Choose a word to practise horizontal joins to ascender. Click on the word to make the focus join grey. Children should be able to join all the letters in these words, with the exception of the break letters.

Common errors

- trying to join horizontally to an ascender, making the ascender too short ○b
- making the *e* too narrow and tall

Group work

Introduce the page

- Ask the children to look at the picture and read the words on the page.

Demonstrate the join

Get Up and Go Cover the words in grey and ask the children to come up and show you which letters can be joined in each word. Remind the children that capital letters never join. Can anyone spot the other letters that don't join? (the *r*s and *b* in *wardrobe*)

- If you wish, you can go through an intermediate stage, where you chunk the words before joining them completely.

- Model tracing over the joined words in grey, emphasising the smooth and flowing movement of your hand.

Show Me Children practise writing the joined words. (They can practise chunking the words first if that is more appropriate.)

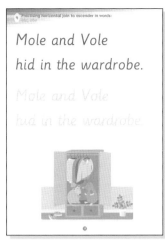

Big Book page 10

Independent work

Encourage the children to read the instruction. ❶ Make sure they chunk the words. If you notice any difficulties, encourage the children to repeat the activity until the chunks are fluent.

Listen to the children read the sentence. ❷ Ask them to spot which letters aren't joined. Make sure they attempt to join the appropriate parts of each word with a fluid movement.

Encourage the children to practise the pattern in the bottom panel.

Can the children Look, Say, Cover, Write and Check these words?

Practice Book page 10

Take away

① For additional practice of this join use **PCM 9**.

② For additional practice of this group of joins use **Year 1 PCMs 28 and 29** (introducing and practising horizontal join to ascender).

10 Practising horizontal join to ascender in words: *ook, ool*

Warm up

- Children put their fingertips together to make a roof, which they hold above their heads. They then put their elbows together to make a V shape. Repeat several times.
- Children repeat the exercise above, but on a smaller scale, making just their hands into a roof rather than their whole arms, and putting their wrists rather than their elbows together to make a V shape.

CD-ROM

Unit focus: joining *ook, ool*.
Phonics and spelling links: short vowel phoneme **oo**; reinforcing long vowel phoneme **ue**.

Artwork
The picture illustrates a word from the word bank. Children identify the word and find the target letter pattern.

Join animations
The letter patterns demonstrate the horizontal join to ascender. Reinforce the flowing movement in this familiar join. Check that letter height and appropriate spacing are maintained.

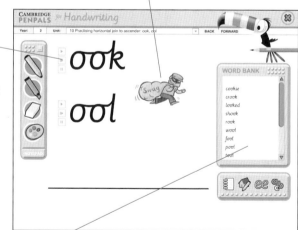

Word bank
Choose a word to practise horizontal joins to ascender. Click on the word to make the focus join grey. Children should be able to join all the letters in these words, with the exception of the break letters.

Common errors
- incorrect relative heights (trying to join horizontally and making the *k* or *l* too small)
- joining capital letters

26

Group work

NB: *s* is not joined to at this stage; joins to *s* will be dealt with later.

Introduce the page
- Ask the children to look at the picture and read the words on the page.

Demonstrate the join
Get Up and Go Cover the words in grey and ask the children to come up and show you which letters can be joined in each word. Remind the children that capital letters never join. Can anyone spot the other letters that don't join? (the *r* in *We're*, the *b* and *s* in *books*, the *s* in *this* and the *s* in *school*)
- If you wish, you can go through an intermediate stage, where you chunk the words before joining them completely.
- Model tracing over the joined words in grey, emphasising the smooth and flowing movement of your hand.
Show Me Children practise writing the joined words. (They can practise chunking the words first if that is more appropriate.)

> We're hooked on books in this school.

Big Book page 11

Independent work

Encourage the children to read the instruction. **①** Make sure they chunk the words. If you notice any difficulties, encourage the children to repeat the activity until the chunks are fluent.

Listen to the children read the sentence. Ask them to spot **②** which letters aren't joined. Make sure they attempt to join the appropriate parts of each word with a fluid movement. If appropriate, point out the shared cross bar on the double *t*.

Encourage the children to practise the pattern in the bottom panel. **③**

Can the children Look, Say, Cover, Write and Check these words?

④

Practice Book page 11

Take away

① For additional practice of this join use **PCM 10**.

② For additional practice of this group of joins use **Year 1 PCMs 28 and 29** (introducing and practising horizontal join to ascender).

11 Practising diagonal join to r: *ir, ur, er*

Warm up

🖐 Children wriggle, stretch, stiffen and relax their arms.
🖐 Children repeat the above with their fingers.

CD-ROM

Unit focus: joining *ir, ur, er.*
Phonics and spelling link: vowel phoneme **er**.

Artwork
The picture illustrates words from the word bank. Children identify the words (e.g. dirt, girl, shirt) and find the target letter patterns.

Join animations
The letter patterns demonstrate the diagonal join to *r*. Reinforce the flowing movement in this familiar join. Check that letter height and appropriate spacing are maintained.

Word bank
Choose a word to practise diagonal joins to *r*. Click on the word to make the focus join grey. Children should be able to join all the letters in these words, with the exception of the break letters.

Common errors

- exaggerating the arch on the *r*
- slanting letters

Group work

Introduce the page
- Identify the letter patterns at the top of the page. Look at the picture and read the sentences.

Demonstrate the join
- Model how to form the letter patterns at the top of the page.
- Model tracing over the letters in grey, emphasising the smooth and flowing movement of your hand.
- Ask children which letter patterns are needed to complete the remaining words.
- Model how to complete the words, being sure to join the new letter pattern to the previous letter where appropriate. Do not join from the break letters (*r, p* or to *s*).

  Show Me Children practise writing these words. (They can practise chunking the words first if that is more appropriate.)

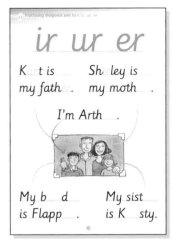

Big Book page 12

Independent work

Watch while children copy the letter patterns, ❶ offering support as necessary.

Encourage the children to read the instructions. Make sure ❷ they understand they have to pair up the words according to the three letter patterns. (*First-aider* goes with *birdwatcher, teacher* with *farmer, burglar* with *nurse*. Can the children tell you which other letter pattern *first-aider* and *birdwatcher* have in common?) Children should chunk the words first if they need to. If you notice any difficulties, encourage the children to repeat the activity until the chunks are fluent. Ask the children if they can spot another join to *r*. (*a* to *r* in *farmer* and *burglar*)

Practice Book page 12

Encourage the children to practise the pattern in the bottom panel. ❸

Can the children Look, Say, Cover, Write and Check these words?

Take away

① For additional practice of this join use **PCM 11**.

② For additional practice of this group of joins use **Year 1 PCMs 15–17** (introducing and practising diagonal join, no ascender).

12 Practising horizontal join to r: *or*, *oor*

Warm up

 Children straighten their arms out to the front, clench their fists and pull the fists towards them. Repeat over the head.

 Children make their fingers gallop.

CD-ROM

Unit focus: joining *or*, *oor*.
Phonics and spelling link: vowel phoneme **or**.

Artwork
The picture illustrates a word from the word bank. Children identify the word and find the target letter pattern.

Join animations
The letter patterns demonstrate the horizontal join to *r*. Reinforce the flowing movement in this familiar join. Check that letter height and appropriate spacing are maintained.

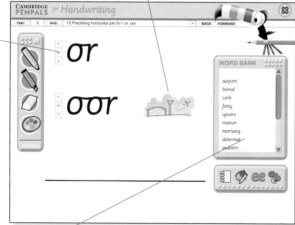

Word bank
Choose a word to practise horizontal joins to *r*. Click on the word to make the focus join grey. Children should be able to join all the letters in these words, with the exception of the break letters.

Common errors
● confusion between *or* and *ov*

Group work

Introduce the page
● Identify the letter patterns at the top of the page, look at the picture and read through the rhyme.

Demonstrate the join
● Model how to form the letter patterns at the top of the page. **Get Up and Go** Ask children to come up and point to the words in the rhyme which contain the *or* and *oor* letter patterns.

● Model tracing over these words in red, emphasising the smooth and flowing movement of your hand.

● Point out the *ve* join in *never*. The join is horizontal and needs to slope down to the starting point of the *e*.

Show Me Children practise writing the *or* and *oor* words. (They can practise chunking the words first if that is more appropriate.)

---

or oor

There was a poor man
 on the moor,
Who wanted to find
 a red door.
He rode a poor horse,
That's true of course,
But he never did find
 that red door!

Big Book page 13

Independent work

Watch while children copy the letter patterns, ❶ offering support as necessary.

Encourage the children to read the instruction ❷ and watch as they copy the sign. Children should chunk the words first if they need to. If you notice any difficulties, encourage the children to repeat the activity until the chunks are fluent.

Encourage the children to practise the pattern in the bottom panel. ❹ ❸

Can the children Look, Say, Cover, Write and Check these words?

Practice Book page 13

Take away

① For additional practice of this join use **PCM 12**.

② For additional practice of this group of joins use **Year 1 PCMs 24 and 25** (introducing and practising horizontal join, no ascender).

13 Introducing horizontal join from r to ascender: *url, irl, irt*

Warm up

- 👋 Children make their arms curl and twirl.
- 👋 Children make their fingers and hands curl and twirl.

CD-ROM

Unit focus: joining *url, irl, irt*.
Phonics and spelling link: vowel phoneme **er**.

Artwork

The picture illustrates a word from the word bank. Children identify the word and find the target letter pattern.

Join animations

The letter patterns demonstrate the horizontal join from *r* to ascender. Reinforce the flowing movement in this join. Check that letter height and appropriate spacing are maintained.

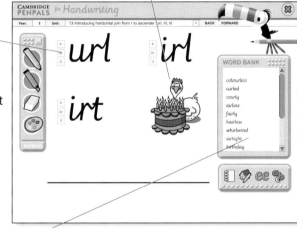

Word bank

Choose a word to practise horizontal joins from *r* to ascender. Click on the word to make the focus join grey. Children should be able to join all the letters in these words, with the exception of the break letters.

Common errors

- not following the line in the retracing of the *u*
- slanting the arch of the *r* rather than using a correctly angled join
- horizonal join from *v* to *e* not dipping down to the starting point of the *e*

Group work

Introduce the page

- Identify the letter patterns at the top of the page, look at the picture and read through the letter.

Demonstrate the join

- Model how to form the letter patterns at the top of the page.
- Talk about the way the *r* dips down before it goes up for the join.

  Get Up and Go Ask children to come up and point to the words containing *url, irl* and *irt* in the letter.

- Model tracing over these words in red, emphasising the smooth and flowing movement of your hand.

  Show Me Children practise writing these words. (They can practise chunking the words first if that is more appropriate.)

Big Book page 14

Independent work

Watch while children copy the letter patterns, ❶ offering support as necessary.

Encourage the children to read the instruction ❷ and watch as they copy the poem. Children should chunk the words first if they need to. If you notice any difficulties, encourage the children to repeat the activity until the chunks are fluent.

Practice Book page 14

Encourage the children to practise the pattern in the bottom panel.

Can the children Look, Say, Cover, Write and Check these words?

Take away

① For additional practice of this join use **PCM 13**.

② For additional practice of this group of joins use **Year 1 PCMs 28 and 29** (introducing and practising horizontal join to ascender).

14 Introducing horizontal join from r: *ere*

Warm up

- Children play 'Point to the …' (left, right, ceiling, floor, door, etc., following your instructions).
- Children bend and stretch each finger in turn. Finish off with a whole-hand stretch.

CD-ROM

Unit focus: joining *ere*.
Phonics and spelling link: vowel phoneme **air**.

Artwork
The picture illustrates a word from the word bank. Children identify the word and find the target letter pattern.

Join animation
The letter pattern demonstrates the horizontal join from *r*. Reinforce the flowing movement in this join. Check that letter height and appropriate spacing are maintained.

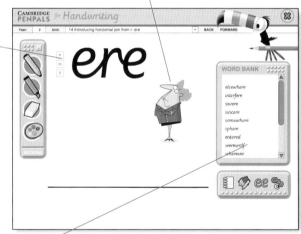

Word bank
Choose a word to practise horizontal joins from *r*. Click on the word to make the focus join grey. Children should be able to join all the letters in these words, with the exception of the break letters.

Common errors
- extending the *r* to look like an *n*
- allowing letters to float above the line

Group work

Introduce the page
- Identify the letter pattern at the top of the page, look at the picture and read the words.

Demonstrate the join
- Model how to form the letter pattern at the top of the page.
- Talk about the way the *r* dips down even further to join the *e*, but it doesn't dip down to join to other short letters (e.g. *r* to *y* in *everywhere*).
- Model tracing over the words in grey, emphasising the smooth and flowing movement of your hand.
  Show Me Children complete the words *anywhere* and *nowhere*. (They can practise chunking them first if that is appropriate.)
- Model how to complete the words correctly, making sure you join the *ere* to the rest of the word.
- As an additional teaching point, look at the apostrophe in *we're* on the top line.

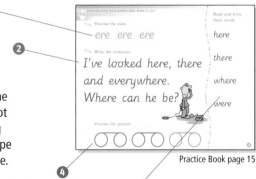

Big Book page 15

Independent work

Watch while children copy the letter pattern, offering support as necessary.

Encourage the children to read the instruction and watch as they copy the sentences. Children should chunk the words first if they need to. If you notice any difficulties, encourage the children to repeat the activity until the chunks are fluent. Can anyone spot another join from *r* to a letter other than *e*? (*r* to *y* in *everywhere*) Discuss that this is the same join type as *r* to *e*, even though the join to *e* dips down more.

Encourage the children to practise the pattern in the bottom panel.

Can the children Look, Say, Cover, Write and Check these high-frequency words?

Practice Book page 15

Take away

① For additional practice of this join use **PCM 14**.

② For additional practice of this group of joins use **Year 1 PCMs 24 and 25** (introducing and practising horizontal join, no ascender).

15 Practising joining to and from r: *air*

Warm up

👋 Children sit on one hand and wave the other. Release. Then push one shoulder back and down, repeating with the other shoulder. Finally, children shrug alternate shoulders.

👋 Children tap each finger in turn on the palm of the opposite hand.

CD-ROM

Unit focus: joining *air*.

Phonics and spelling links: vowel phoneme **air**; compound words.

Artwork

The picture illustrates a word from the word bank. Children identify the word and find the target letter pattern.

Join animation

The letter pattern demonstrates joining to *r*. Reinforce the flowing movement in these joins. Check that letter height and appropriate spacing are maintained.

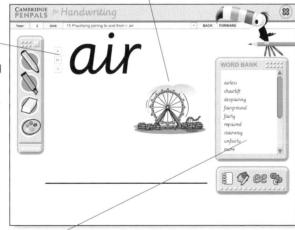

Word bank

Choose a word to practise joining to and from *r*. Click on the word to make the focus join grey. Children should be able to join all the letters in these words, with the exception of the break letters.

Common errors

- not making the stalk of the *a* long enough, misshaping the *i*
- joining from the top of the *i* to the *r*

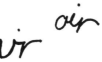

Group work

Introduce the page

- Identify the letter pattern at the top of the page. Make sure children understand that they are going to be making compound words with *air* in them.

Demonstrate the join

- Model how to form the letter pattern at the top of the page.
- Trace over the word *airfield*, emphasising the smooth and flowing movement of your hand. Note that the *r* to *f* join is similar to the joins introduced in Unit 13. You may also wish to refer back to Y1/P2 Unit 30 (Introducing horizontal and diagonal joins, to ascender, to an anticlockwise letter: joining *of*, *if*).
- Ask children to tell you which word beginning with *air* should be written next to each picture. (*aircraft, airport, airmail, airman*)

  Show Me Children practise writing the words themselves.
- You may wish to point out the different spelling of *aeroplane*.

Big Book page 16

Independent work

Watch while children copy the letter pattern, offering support as necessary.

Encourage the children to read the instruction. Make sure they understand how the word web works and watch as they write the words. Make sure that the children join the *r* to the first letter of the ending. Children should chunk the words first if they need to. If you notice any difficulties, encourage the children to repeat the activity until the chunks are fluent.

Encourage the children to practise the pattern in the bottom panel.

Can the children Look, Say, Cover, Write and Check these words?

Practice Book page 16

Take away

① For additional practice of this join use **PCM 15**.

② For additional practice of this group of joins use **Year 1 PCMs 15–17** (introducing and practising diagonal join, no ascender) or **Year 1 PCMs 24–30** (introducing and practising horizontal join, no ascender/to ascender).

16 Introducing diagonal join to s: *dis*

Warm up

☝ Children make a V with two flat hands and rest their chin on it. Then they make an inverted V with flat hands and put it over their head like a roof.

☝ Children shake first one hand, then the other.

CD-ROM

Unit focus: joining *dis*.

Phonics and spelling link: prefix **dis**.

Artwork

The picture illustrates a word from the word bank. Children identify the word and find the target letter pattern.

Join animation

The letter pattern demonstrates the diagonal join to *s*. Introduce the new shape of the *s* when it is being joined. Reinforce the flowing movement in this join. Clarify that letter height and appropriate spacing are maintained.

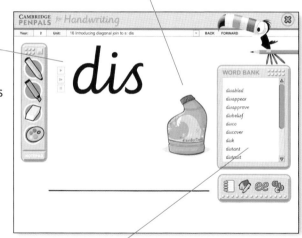

Word bank

Choose a word to practise diagonal joins to *s*. Click on the word to make the focus join grey. Introduce the new *s* in the context of a word.

Common errors

● drawing a jagged *s*, like a back-to-front *z*

● curve of *s* falling below the line

Group work

Introduce the page

● Identify the letter pattern at the top of the page. Look at the pictures and read the words. The text in the speech bubbles offers an opportunity to discuss capitals.

● Make sure children understand the meaning of the prefix *dis* and how it changes the meaning of a word (makes it negative).

Demonstrate the join

● Model how to form the letter pattern at the top of the page. Talk children through the *i* to *s* join, explaining that you go up to the top as if you were going to write a letter *c*, then fit in two little curves to make an *s*.

● Note that the top curve of a joined-to *s* is shallower than an unjoined *s*.

● Trace over the word *dislike*, emphasising the smooth and flowing movement of your hand.

● Model writing *dis* in the next gap to create the word *disagree*.
Show Me Children practise adding *dis* to the remaining words.

● Model writing up the last two words correctly. Make sure children see that the *e* to *s* join in *dishonest* is made in the same way as the *i* to *s* join.

Big Book page 17

Independent work

Watch while children copy the letter pattern, offering support as necessary.

Encourage the children to read the instruction and watch while they copy the sentences. Children should chunk the words first if they need to. If you notice any difficulties, encourage the children to repeat the activity until the chunks are fluent.

Encourage the children to practise the pattern in the bottom panel.

Can the children Look, Say, Cover, Write and Check these high-frequency words?

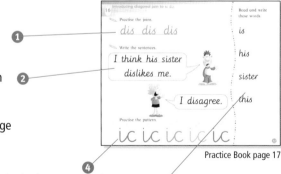

Practice Book page 17

Take away

① For additional practice of this join use **PCM 16**.

② For additional practice of a similar group of joins use **Year 1 PCMs 18–20** (introducing and practising diagonal join, no ascender, to an anticlockwise letter).

17 Introducing horizontal join to s: ws

Warm up

👐 Children move their arms in and out and cross them, turn them over palms up, bend their elbows and wiggle their thumbs.

👐 Children spread their fingers and match them up to the fingers of the opposite hand. Then push the palms together and open them out again.

CD-ROM

Unit focus: joining ws.
Phonics and spelling link: practising handwriting in conjunction with phonics and spelling work.

Artwork
The picture illustrates a word from the word bank. Children identify the word and find the target letter pattern.

Join animation
The letter pattern demonstrates the horizontal join to s. Reinforce the new shape of the s when it is being joined and the flowing movement in the join. Clarify that letter height and appropriate spacing are maintained.

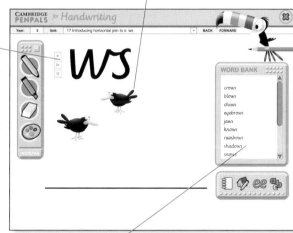

Word bank
Choose a word to practise horizontal joins to s. Click on the word to make the focus join grey. Introduce the new shape of the s in the context of a word.

Common errors
- joining diagonally up from the w to the s, making the s too large
- backing the s up against the w so the letters are intertwined

Group work

Introduce the page
- Identify the letter pattern at the top of the page. Look at the newspaper page and read the words.

Demonstrate the join
- Model how to form the letter pattern at the top of the page. Talk children through the w to s join, explaining that you go straight across as if you were going to write a letter c, then fit in two little curves to make an s.
  Get Up and Go Ask children to come up and point to the ws patterns in the words on the page.
- Model tracing the words containing the ws pattern (in red).
  Show Me Children practise writing these words.

Big Book page 18

Independent work

Watch while children copy the letter pattern, ❶ offering support as necessary.

Encourage the children to read the instruction ❷ and watch while they copy the phrases. Children should chunk the words first if they need to. If you notice any difficulties, encourage the children to repeat the activity until the chunks are fluent.

Encourage the children to practise the pattern in the bottom panel. ❹ ❸

Can the children Look, Say, Cover, Write and Check these words?

Practice Book page 18

Take away

① For additional practice of this join use **PCM 17**.

② For additional practice of a similar group of joins use **Year 1 PCMs 26 and 27** (introducing and practising horizontal join, no ascender, to an anticlockwise letter).

18 Introducing diagonal join from s to ascender: *sh*

- Children mime a sunrise with their arms.
- Children mime a sunrise with their hands.

CD-ROM

Unit focus: joining *sh*.
Phonics and spelling link: practising handwriting in conjunction with phonics and spelling work.

Artwork
The picture illustrates a word from the word bank. Children identify the word and find the target letter pattern.

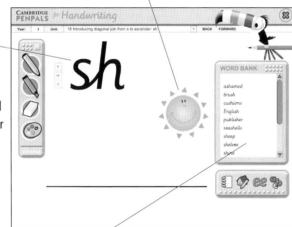

Join animation
The letter pattern demonstrates the diagonal join from *s* to ascender. Introduce the join from *s* by exploring where it starts and the path it takes. Check that letter height and appropriate spacing are maintained.

Word bank
Choose a word to practise diagonal joins from *s* to ascender. Click on the word to make the focus join grey. Check that joins to and from *s* are flowing and controlled.

Common errors
- making *h* too small so it looks like an *n*
- forgetting the stalk on the *h* and adding it afterwards

sh

Group work

Introduce the page
- Identify the letter pattern at the top of the page. Identify *sh* as a digraph like *ch* and *th*. Look at the picture and read the rules.

Demonstrate the join
- Model how to form the letter pattern at the top of the page. Talk children through the join, explaining that after you've written the *s* you swing back round and up to the top of the *h*.
- Ask children to find another letter with an ascender to which *s* joins to an ascender. (*t* in *first*)

  Get Up and Go Ask children to come up and point to the *sh* letter patterns in the words on the page.
- Model tracing the words containing the *sh* pattern.
  Show Me Children practise writing these words.
- Can anyone think of one more rule involving a word with the *sh* letter pattern in it? (e.g. *No fishing, No ships*) Model writing it as rule number six.

Ashby Pool Rules
1. No pushing.
2. No shouting.
3. No shoving.
4. No splashing.
5. Have a shower first.
6.

Big Book page 19

Independent work

Watch while children copy the letter pattern, offering support as necessary.

Encourage the children to read the instruction and watch while they copy the sentence. Children should chunk the words first if they need to. If you notice any difficulties, encourage the children to repeat the activity until the chunks are fluent.

Encourage the children to practise the pattern in the bottom panel.

Can the children Look, Say, Cover, Write and Check these words?

Practise the join.
sh sh sh
Write the sentence.
Splashing sunshine makes shadows shift and shapes shimmer.
Practise the pattern.

Read and write these words.
push
should
shop
shape

Practice Book page 19

Take away

① For additional practice of this join use **PCM 18**.

② For additional practice of a similar group of joins use **Year 1 PCMs 11–14** (introducing and practising diagonal join to ascender).

19 Introducing diagonal join from s, no ascender: *si, su, se, sp, sm*

Warm up

👋 Children make large waves with their arms, first with one arm and then with both together, making them flow in and out, to the left and to the right.

👋 Starting at the wrist, children draw wiggly snakes with their index fingers across their palm and right up to the end of each finger. Repeat with the opposite hand.

CD-ROM

Unit focus: joining *si, su, se, sp, sm.*
Phonics and spelling links: compound words; practising handwriting in conjunction with phonics and spelling work.

Artwork
The picture illustrates a word from the word bank. Children identify the word and find the target letter pattern.

Join animations
The letter patterns demonstrate the diagonal join from *s*, no ascender. Introduce the join from *s* by exploring where it starts and the path it takes. Check that letter height and appropriate spacing are maintained.

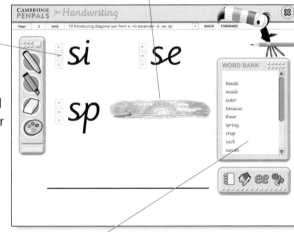

Word bank
Choose a word to practise diagonal joins from *s*, no ascender. Click on the word to make the focus join grey. Check that joins to and from *s* are flowing and controlled.

Common errors
- stretching the join so that letters are too far apart
- joining too horizontally so that the second letter falls below the line

35

Group work

Introduce the page
- Identify the letter patterns at the top of the page.
- Explain to children that in this activity, they need to match up the two halves of some common phrases.

Demonstrate the join
- Model how to form the letter patterns at the top of the page. Talk children through the join, explaining that after you've written the *s* you swing back round and up to the top of the second letter. You may wish to look at the *se* join separately, showing children how, after they have come back round, they swing straight into the loop of the *e*.
- Model tracing over the letter patterns in grey. Also model how the pattern joins on to the rest of the word where appropriate.
- Ask children to match up the words to make phrases. (*spick and span, smashed to smithereens, house mouse, sing for your supper, sixes and sevens*)
  Show Me Children practise writing words containing the target letter patterns.

Independent work

Watch while children copy the letter patterns, ➊ offering support as necessary.

Encourage the children to read the instruction. Make sure ➋ they understand that they have to match up one word from each column to make compound words. Children should chunk the words first if they need to. If you notice any difficulties, encourage the children to repeat the activity until the chunks are fluent. Check that joins to *s* are correctly formed.

Encourage the children to practise the pattern in the bottom panel. ➌

Can the children Look, Say, Cover, Write and Check these words?

Big Book page 20

Practice Book page 20

Take away

① For additional practice of this join use **PCM 19**.

② For additional practice of a similar group of joins use **Year 1 PCMs 15–17** (introducing and practising diagonal join, no ascender).

Warm up

☝ Children make large spirals with their arms, first with one arm and then with both together. They then change direction.

☝ Children make spirals with their fingers, changing direction from time to time.

Unit focus: joining *rs*.

Phonics and spelling link: practising handwriting in conjunction with phonics and spelling work.

Artwork

The picture illustrates a word from the word bank. Children identify the word and find the target letter pattern.

Join animation

The letter pattern demonstrates the horizontal join from *r* to an anticlockwise letter. Clarify that both *r* and *s* have a new joined form. Check that letter height and appropriate spacing are maintained.

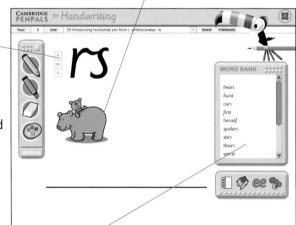

Word bank

Choose a word to practise horizontal joins from *r* to an anticlockwise letter. Click on the word to make the focus join grey. Check that joins from *r* are flowing and controlled.

Common errors

- merging the *r* and the *s* *rs*
- making the *r* into an *n* and missing the join

Group work

Introduce the page

- Identify the letter pattern at the top of the page. Read the mnemonic aloud in a rhythmic way (*Mrs D, Mrs I, Mrs FFI*, etc.) and explain to children that it is a way to help you remember the spelling of *difficulty*.

Demonstrate the join

- Model how to form the letter pattern at the top of the page. Talk children through the join, explaining that you need to dip down slightly when writing the arm of the *r*. You then go straight across to the top of the *s* and write it as usual. Children may find it helpful to sky write this letter pattern before they practise writing it. Other anticlockwise letters joined in this way are *c*, *a*, *d*, *g* and *o*. Note that the children have already met *r* to *f* in Unit 15.
- Model tracing over the letter pattern in grey.
- Model writing the letter pattern in the spaces.
  Show Me Children practise writing *Mrs* themselves.

Big Book page 21

Independent work

Watch while children copy the letter pattern, ❶ offering support as necessary.

Encourage the children to read the speech bubbles, ❷ following each row left to right. Watch as children write the words. (They should chunk the words first if they need to.) If you notice any difficulties, encourage the children to repeat the activity until the chunks are fluent. Note that there is no join between *t* and *s* in *it's* because of the apostrophe.

Encourage the children to practise the pattern in the bottom panel. ❸

Can the children Look, Say, Cover, Write and Check these words?

Practice Book page 21

Take away

① For additional practice of this join use **PCM 20**.

② For additional practice of a similar group of joins use **Year 1 PCMs 24 and 25** (introducing and practising horizontal join, no ascender).

21 Practising diagonal join to an anticlockwise letter: *ea, ear*

Warm up

👆 Children try to make their shoulder touch their ear. Repeat on the other side.
👆 Children put their wrists together, then their palms and fingertips. Repeat with the backs of the hands.

CD-ROM

Unit focus: joining *ea, ear*.
Phonics and spelling link: phonemes **ea** and **ear**.

Artwork
The picture illustrates a word from the word bank. Children identify the word and find the target letter pattern.

Join animations
The letter patterns demonstrate the diagonal join to an anticlockwise letter. Focus on the flow throughout the join. Check the shape of all the letters. Check that letter height and appropriate spacing are maintained.

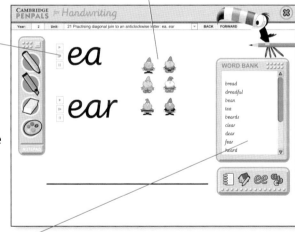

Word bank
Choose a word to practise diagonal joins to an anticlockwise letter. Click on the word to make the focus join grey. Check that all joins are flowing and controlled, and that the size and spacing of letters is consistent.

Common errors
● not reversing back accurately on the *a*
● letting the *a* and *r* float above the line

ear

Group work

Introduce the page
● Identify the letter patterns at the top of the page. Read the words and look at the pictures.

Demonstrate the join
● Model how to form the letter patterns at the top of the page.
● Model tracing over the letter patterns in grey, making sure that you go on to join the *r* to the *w* in *earwig* and the *r* to the *p* in *earphones*.
● Model writing the letter pattern in the spaces, again making sure that you join the whole word where appropriate.
● Remind children that they have already met the join from *r* to an anticlockwise letter in Unit 20 – the joins from *r* to *a* and *r* to *d* are similar.

Show Me Children practise writing the words themselves.

Big Book page 22

Independent work

Watch while children copy the letter patterns, **❶** offering support as necessary.

Encourage the children to read the rhyme. Watch **❷** while children write the words. (They should chunk the words first if they need to.) If you notice any difficulties, encourage the children to repeat the activity until the chunks are fluent.

Encourage the children to practise the pattern in the bottom panel. **❸**

Can the children Look, Say, Cover, Write and Check these words? **❹**

Practice Book page 22

Take away

① For additional practice of this join use **PCM 21**.

② For additional practice of this group of joins use **Year 1 PCMs 18–20** (introducing and practising diagonal join, no ascender, to an anticlockwise letter).

22 Introducing horizontal join from f to ascender: *ft, fl*

Warm up

- Children move their arms up and down gently like wings. They then move their arms more stiffly like the hands of a clock.
- Children make little butterflies with their hands, making them fly in different directions.

CD-ROM

Unit focus: joining *ft, fl*.

Phonics and spelling link: practising handwriting in conjunction with phonics and spelling work.

Artwork
The picture illustrates a word from the word bank. Children identify the word and find the target letter pattern.

Join animations
The letter patterns demonstrate the join from *f* to ascender. Focus on the fact that the *f* joins from its crossbar. Check the shape of all the letters. Check that ascenders and descenders are appropriate, and that appropriate spacing is maintained.

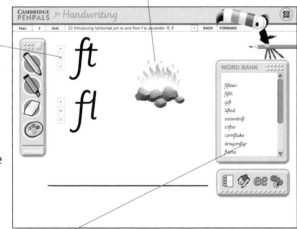

Word bank
Choose a word to practise joining from *f* to ascender. Click on the word to make the focus join grey. Check that all joins are flowing and controlled and that the size and spacing of letters is consistent.

Common errors
- placing the crossbar too low down on the *f*
- placing the crossbar at a sharp diagonal

Group work

Introduce the page
- Identify the letter patterns at the top of the page. Read the words and look at the picture.

Demonstrate the join
- Model how to form the letter patterns at the top of the page. Talk children through how to make the join, showing them how you put the crossbar on the *f* and carry it on straight across and then up to the top of the next letter.
  Get Up and Go Ask children to come up and point to words containing the *ft* and *fl* patterns.
- Model how to write the words containing the letter patterns.
- Although children have met joins similar to the *ef* (diagonal join to ascender, e.g. *el*) and the *rf* (horizontal join to ascender, e.g. *of*), you may wish to give them the opportunity for extra practice of these joins.
  Show Me Children practise writing these words themselves.

ft   fl

*Flutter by butterfly,
flap to the left,
flit to the right.
Bye, bye butterfly.*

Big Book page 23

Independent work

Watch while children copy the letter patterns, offering support as necessary. **1**

Encourage the children to read the sentences. **2** Watch while children write the words. (They should chunk the words first if they need to.) If you notice any difficulties, encourage the children to repeat the activity until the chunks are fluent.

Encourage the children to practise the pattern in the bottom panel. **4**

Can the children Look, Say, Cover, Write and Check these words?

Practice Book page 23

Take away

① For additional practice of this join use **PCM 22**.

② For additional practice of a similar group of joins use **Year 1 PCMs 28 and 29** (introducing and practising horizontal join to ascender).

23 Introducing horizontal join from f, no ascender: *fu*, *fr*

Warm up

- 👋 Children shrug their right and then their left shoulder.
- 👋 Children grip one hand in the other, then shake them out.

CD-ROM

Unit focus: joining *fu*, *fr*.
Phonics and spelling link: practising handwriting in conjunction with phonics and spelling work.

Artwork
The picture illustrates a word from the word bank. Children identify the word and find the target letter pattern.

Join animations
The letter patterns demonstrate the horizontal join from *f*, no ascender. Focus on the fact that the *f* joins from its crossbar. Check the shape of all the letters. Check that ascenders and descenders are appropriate, and that appropriate spacing is maintained.

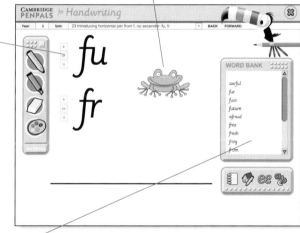

Word bank
Choose a word to practise horizontal joins from *f*, no ascender. Click on the word to make the focus join grey. Check that all joins are flowing and controlled and that the size and spacing of letters is consistent.

Common errors
- placing the crossbar too low down on the *f*
- standing the *f* on the line, with no descender below the line   *fr*

Group work

Introduce the page
- Identify the letter patterns at the top of the page. Read the sentence and look at the picture.

Demonstrate the join
- Model how to form the letter patterns at the top of the page. Talk children through how to make the join, showing them how you put the crossbar on the *f* and carry it on straight across to the top of the next letter. Notice the same applies when joining to anticlockwise letters (e.g. *f* to *o* in *four-legged*).
  Get Up and Go Ask children to come up and point to words containing the *fu* and *fr* patterns.
- Model how to trace the words containing the letter patterns.
  Show Me Children practise writing these words themselves.

fu   fr

My four-legged friend is full of fun and frolics.

Big Book page 24

Independent work

Watch while children copy the letter patterns, offering support as necessary. ❶

Encourage the children to read the first sentence. ❷ Watch while they write the words. (They should chunk the words first if they need to.) If you notice any difficulties, encourage the children to repeat the activity until the chunks are fluent.

Ask the children to write their friends' names in the gaps. ❸

Encourage the children to practise the pattern in the bottom panel. ❺

Can the children Look, Say, Cover, Write and Check these words?

Practice Book page 24

Take away

① For additional practice of this join use **PCM 23**.

② For additional practice of a similar group of joins use **Year 1 PCMs 24 and 25** (introducing and practising horizontal join, no ascender).

24 Introducing *qu* (diagonal join, no ascender)

Big Book page 25

What's the opposite of ...

loud?

king?

answer?

solid?

Warm up

- Children circle their arms forwards and then backwards.
- Children tap their fist against the palm of their hand. Then repeat with the other hand. They can make up a rhythm.

CD-ROM

Unit focus: joining *qu*.
Phonics and spelling link: practising handwriting in conjunction with phonics and spelling work.

Artwork
The picture illustrates a word from the word bank. Children identify the word and find the target letter pattern.

Join animation
The letter pattern demonstrates the join from *q* to *u*. Focus on the fact that the *q* joins from its flick. Check the shape of both the letters. Check that the descender is appropriate, and that appropriate spacing is maintained.

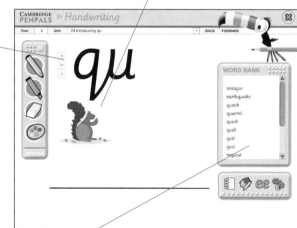

Word bank
Choose a word to practise joining *q* to *u*. Click on the word to make the focus join grey. Check that all joins are flowing and controlled and that the size and spacing of letters is consistent.

Common errors
- not continuing the flick of the *q* far enough
- sending the flick of the *q* out at a right angle under the line

Group work

Introduce the page
- Identify the letter pattern at the top of the page. Read the words and look at the pictures. Explain to the children that they are going to be thinking of words that have *qu* in them (not strictly opposites for the nouns).
- Talk about the formation of the question mark.

Demonstrate the join
- Model how to form the letter pattern at the top of the page. Talk children through how to make the join, showing them how to continue the flick on the tail of the *q* right up to the top of the *u*.
- Ask children to suggest the opposite of the words given – a clue is that they all have *qu* in them. (The answers are *quiet*, *queen*, *question*, *liquid*.)
- Model how to trace the words. If appropriate, you could ask children to suggest the spellings.
  Show Me Children practise writing the words themselves.

Independent work

Watch while children copy the letter pattern, offering support as necessary.

Encourage the children to read the sentence. Watch while they write the words. (They should chunk the words first if they need to.) If you notice any difficulties, encourage the children to repeat the activity until the chunks are fluent.

Encourage the children to practise the pattern in the bottom panel.

Can the children Look, Say, Cover, Write and Check these words?

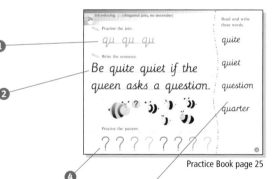

Practice Book page 25

Take away

① For additional practice of this join use **PCM 24**.

② For additional practice of a similar group of joins use **Year 1 PCMs 15–17** (introducing and practising diagonal join, no ascender).

25 Introducing *rr* (horizontal join, no ascender)

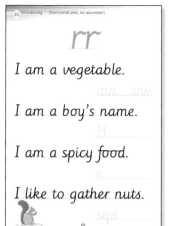

Big Book page 26

Warm up

- Children stretch their arms out in front with fingers locked. They lean forward from the waist and push their hands away, stretching their shoulders and back. They then put their arms behind their body, again with fingers interlocking, and stretch.
- Children wriggle their fingers as if scrabbling in the ground for nuts like a squirrel. They turn their hands over (palms up) and repeat with fingers pointing upwards.

CD-ROM

Unit focus: joining *rr*.

Phonics and spelling link: practising handwriting in conjunction with phonics and spelling work.

Artwork

The picture illustrates a word from the word bank. Children identify the word and find the target letter pattern.

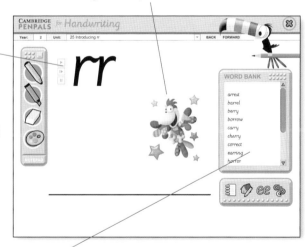

Join animation

The letter pattern demonstrates the *rr* join, horizontal, no ascender. Focus on the fact that each *r* has a joined form. Check the shape of both the letters and that appropriate spacing is maintained.

Word bank

Choose a word to practise joining *rr*. Click on the word to make the focus join grey. Check that all joins are flowing and controlled and that the size and spacing of letters is consistent.

Common errors

- bending the first *r* down too far like an *n*
- making stalks on the *r*s too tall

Group work

Introduce the page

- Identify the letter pattern at the top of the page. Read the clues and explain that children are going to find the answers, all of which have *rr* in them.

Demonstrate the join

- Model how to form the letter pattern at the top of the page. Talk children through how to make the join, showing them how you need to make a little dip at the end of the first *r* before starting the second one. Children may find it helpful to try sky writing the pattern before they practise writing it.
- Trace over the word *marrow*, writing *rr* into the gap. Be sure to join the letter pattern to the letters before and after it.
- Ask children to suggest answers to the remaining clues. Remind them that they all have *rr* in them. (The answers are *Harry, curry* and *squirrel*.)
- Model how to write the words. If appropriate, you could ask children to suggest the spellings.
  Show Me Children practise writing the words themselves.

Independent work

Watch while children copy the letter pattern, offering support as necessary. ❶

Encourage the children to read the address. ❷ Watch while they write the words. (They should chunk the words first if they need to.) If you notice any difficulties, encourage the children to repeat the activity until the chunks are fluent.

Encourage the children to practise the pattern in the bottom panel. ❸

Can the children Look, Say, Cover, Write and Check these words?

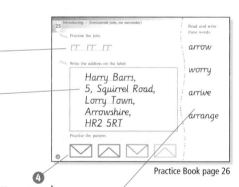

Practice Book page 26

Take away

① For additional practice of this join use **PCM 25**.

② For additional practice of a similar group of joins use **Year 1 PCMs 24 and 25** (introducing and practising horizontal join, no ascender).

26 Introducing _ss_ (diagonal join, no ascender, to an anticlockwise letter)

Warm up

- ✋ Children hold their arms straight out in front of them and criss-cross them in a scissor-like motion while moving them up over their head and back down again.
- ✋ Children criss-cross their fingers – one pair at a time on the same hand. Repeat with the other hand.

CD-ROM

Unit focus: joining _ss_.

Phonics and spelling link: practising handwriting in conjunction with phonics and spelling work.

Artwork
The picture illustrates a word from the word bank. Children identify the word and find the target letter pattern.

Join animation
The letter pattern demonstrates the _ss_ join, diagonal, no ascender, to an anticlockwise letter. Focus on the fact that each _s_ has a joined form. Check the shape of all the letters. Check that appropriate spacing is maintained.

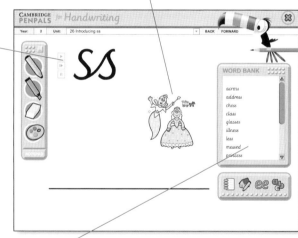

Word bank
Choose a word to practise joining _ss_. Click on the word to make the focus join grey. Check that all joins are flowing and controlled and that the size and spacing of letters is consistent.

Common errors
- writing the second _s_ too loosely so that it almost resembles an _f_
- looping the _s_ as a lazy way of joining it

Group work

NB: Although the specific focus of this unit is _ss_, you might wish to point out to children that a similar joining movement is used to join _s_ to other anticlockwise letters, for example _sa, sc, sd, sg, so, sq._

Introduce the page
- Identify the letter pattern at the top of the page. Read the text.

Demonstrate the join
- Model how to form the letter pattern at the top of the page. Talk children through how to make the join, explaining that after you've written the _s_ you swing back round and up as if you were going to write a _c_. You then need to fit in the two little curves of the _s_. Children may find it helpful to sky write the pattern before they practise writing it.
  Get Up and Go Ask children to come up and point to the words with _ss_ in them.
- Model writing the words with _ss_ in them.
  Show Me Children practise writing the words themselves.

Are you stressed?
Are you hassled?
Don't make a fuss
because you will all
pass the test.

Big Book page 27

Independent work

Watch while children copy the letter pattern, ❶ offering support as necessary.

Encourage the children to read the sentence. ❷ Watch while they write the sentence. (They should chunk the words first if they need to.) If you notice any difficulties, encourage the children to repeat the activity until the chunks are fluent.

Encourage the children to practise the pattern in the bottom panel.
Can the children Look, Say, Cover, Write and Check these words?

Practice Book page 27

Take away

① For additional practice of this join use **PCM 26**.

② For additional practice of a similar group of joins use **Year 1 PCMs 18–20** (introducing and practising diagonal join, no ascender, to an anticlockwise letter).

27 Introducing *ff* (horizontal join to ascender)

Warm up

- Children tuck their elbows into their waists with their forearms out in front and their fingers touching. They then move their forearms out to the side, keeping a right angle at the elbow.
- Children interlock their fingers tightly and then stretch them out. Repeat several times.

CD-ROM

Unit focus: joining *ff*.
Phonics and spelling link: practising handwriting in conjunction with phonics and spelling work.

Artwork

The picture illustrates a word from the word bank. Children identify the word and find the target letter pattern.

Join animation

The letter pattern demonstrates the *ff* join, horizontal to ascender. Focus on the fact that each *f* joins from its crossbar. Check the shape of all the letters. Check that ascenders and descenders are appropriate, and that appropriate spacing is maintained.

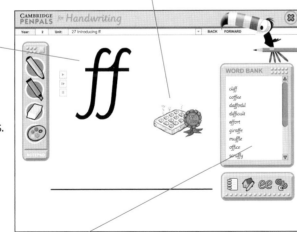

Word bank

Choose a word to practise joining *ff*. Click on the word to make the focus join grey. Check that all joins are flowing and controlled and that the size and spacing of letters is consistent.

Common errors

- not following the curve at the top of the second *f* back properly

Group work

Introduce the page

- Identify the letter pattern at the top of the page. Read the text of the advert.

Demonstrate the join

- Model how to form the letter pattern at the top of the page. Talk children through how to make the join, explaining that after you've written the first *f* you carry on the crossbar straight across and then up to the top of the second *f*. Then you stop and curve back round to finish the second *f* as normal, putting on the crossbar last of all. Children may find it helpful to sky write the pattern before they practise writing it. Notice that in the join from *f* to *e* the crossbar is lower to accommodate the correct starting height of the *e*.

  Get Up and Go Ask children to come up and point to the words with *ff* in them.

- Model writing the words with *ff* in them.

  Show Me Children practise writing the words themselves.

Big Book page 28

Independent work

Watch while children copy the letter pattern, offering support as necessary.

Encourage the children to read the sentences. Watch while they write the sentences. (They should chunk the words first if they need to.) If you notice any difficulties, encourage the children to repeat the activity until the chunks are fluent.

Encourage the children to practise the pattern in the bottom panel.

Can the children Look, Say, Cover, Write and Check these words?

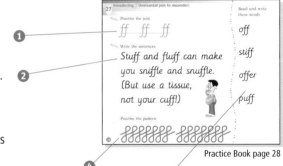

Practice Book page 28

Take away

① For additional practice of this join use **PCM 27**.

② For additional practice of a similar group of joins use **Year 1 PCMs 28 and 29** (introducing and practising horizontal join to ascender).

28 Capital letter practice: height of ascenders and capitals

January   ebruary

arch   pril

ay   une

uly   ugust

September   ctober

ovember   ecember

Big Book page 29

Warm up

- Children rotate each arm forwards and then backwards. Repeat several times.
- Children bend and stretch each finger in turn. They then rotate their hands from the wrist, first one way, then the other.

CD-ROM

Unit focus: height of ascenders and capitals.
Phonics and spelling link: reinforcing spelling of high-frequency words.

Artwork
The picture illustrates two words from the word bank. Children identify the words and find the capital letters.

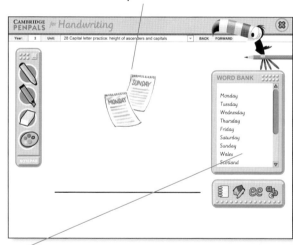

Word bank
Choose a word to practise a range of joins. Click on the word to make the focus join grey. Check that all of the letters including the ascenders and the descenders are of the correct height. Check that all joins are flowing and controlled and that the size and spacing of letters is consistent.

Common errors
- using capital letters in the middle of words
- varying the height of capitals in consecutive words

Group work

Introduce the page
- Identify the fact that this page is all about months of the year. Read out the months in order.

Demonstrate the join
- Ask the children to tell you which letter is needed to complete the name of each month.
- Trace over the word *September.* Ask the children to suggest how tall the capital S should be. (as tall as the letter b) Remind them that capital letters never join. Ask the children what they notice about the t in *September.* (It's a bit shorter than the S and the b.)
- Model writing in the rest of the capitals, asking the children to help you decide how tall each one should be.
  Show Me Children practise writing the words themselves.

Independent work

Watch while children copy the heading, offering support as necessary. ❶

Encourage the children to read the instruction. Watch ❷ while they write the words. (They should chunk the words first if they need to.) If you notice any difficulties, encourage the children to repeat the activity until the chunks are fluent. Keep an eye out for correct sizes of capitals and ascenders. Remind the children that t is always a little shorter than other letters with ascenders.

Encourage the children to practise the pattern in the bottom panel.

Can the children Look, Say, Cover, Write and Check these words?

Write the heading.
MONTHS OF THE YEAR

Write the months of the year.
January February March
April May June July
August September October
November December

Practise the pattern.
MWMWMWM

Read and write these words.
day
week
month
year

Practice Book page 29

❹ ❸

Take away

① For additional practice use **PCM 28**.

② For additional practice of capital letters use **Year 1 PCM 10** (revision of capital letters).

Warm up

👋 Which warm-up activities have the children enjoyed and remembered? Ask individuals to lead the class through their favourite routines and activities.

CD-ROM

Unit focus: teaching criteria for self-assessment.
Phonics and spelling link: practising handwriting in conjunction with phonics and spelling work.

Artwork
The picture shows a toucan holding a pencil to indicate this is the start of the assessment activities.

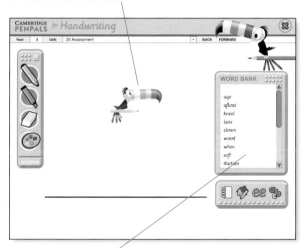

Word bank
Choose a word to practise a range of joins. Click on the word to make the focus join grey. Check that all of the letters including the ascenders and the descenders are of the correct height. Check that all joins are flowing and controlled and that the size and spacing of letters is consistent.

Group work

Introduce the page
- Explain to children that they are going to assess some samples of writing by other Year 2 children.

Demonstrate the unit focus
- Talk about the samples of children's writing on the left-hand page (page 30) of the Big Book. Read the joke together and then ask the children to make comments about any aspect of the handwriting they think is important. Which sample of writing do the children think is the best? Why?
- Read through the statements listed on the right-hand page (page 31). If the children raised any issues that are not broadly addressed here, add them to the bottom of the list. Talk about the fact that these are all important things to think about when assessing handwriting.
- Re-read the statements, one at a time, pausing after each one to decide which of the samples of writing has achieved this aim. Each statement may apply to one or more of the samples. Write the number of the statement beside all the samples to which it applies.
- Once you have considered all the assessment statements, and listed those that apply to each handwriting sample, agree which piece of writing most closely met the list of assessment statements. Is this the sample the children thought was best earlier on? Talk about 'good', neat handwriting.

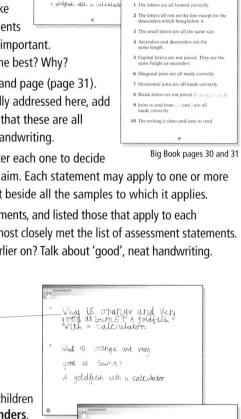

Big Book pages 30 and 31

Independent work

Read the joke together. ❶

Ask the children which of the handwriting ❷ samples they think is the 'best'.

Read the statements together and make sure that the children understand the technical vocabulary, for example **ascenders**, **descenders**, **horizontal join** and **diagonal join**. ❸

The children should try to match each statement against both ❹ samples of writing. They should draw two columns in their handwriting books labelled 'A' and 'B'. They then write the number of each of the statements they choose in the appropriate box. Which box has more statements? Is this handwriting sample the 'best'? Alternatively use PCM 29.

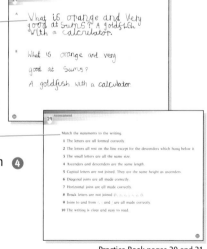

Practice Book pages 30 and 31

Take away

Use **PCM 29** for children to complete a self-assessment of a sample of their own handwriting.

- Teach children a simple routine in which they stretch up high in the air, then put their hands on their heads, shoulders, hips, knees and toes and finally clap.
- Children perform a similar routine to the one above, but this time they stretch their fingers, make fists, wriggle their fingers, bend their thumbs, flop their wrists and finally clap.

CD-ROM

Unit focus: consolidating and assessing work from Y2/P3.
Phonics and spelling link: practising handwriting in conjunction with phonics and spelling work.

Artwork

The picture illustrates some of the words from the word bank. Children identify the words and find the target letter patterns.

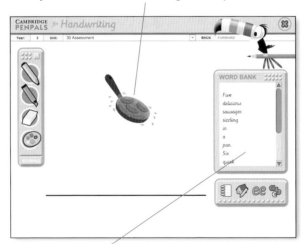

Word bank

Choose a word to practise a range of joins including joining double letters. Click on the word to make it grey. Check that all of the letters including the ascenders and the descenders are of the correct height. Check that all joins are flowing and controlled and that the size and spacing of letters is consistent.

Group work

NB: The Big Book page for this unit (page 32) offers an opportunity to consolidate this year's work. The results of children's Practice Book work can be used as an end-of-year assessment to measure their progress and identify targets for the coming year.

Introduce the page
- Explain that this unit offers a chance to recap joins learnt this year.
- Talk about the punctuation and apostrophes.

Demonstrate the unit focus
- Read the sentence at the top of the page.
- Which break letters can the children find in the sentence? (b in *brown*, p in *jumped*, x in *fox* and z in *lazy*) Model tracing over the sentence, emphasising the fluid movement of your hand.
- Read the joke. Ask the children to tell you which letters should be the tallest (the capitals and letters with ascenders – these should all be the same height). Which letter with an ascender is the odd one out? (t)
  Get Up and Go Ask children to come up and point to the break letter (j in *joke*).
- Model tracing over the joke. Make sure children realise that if a word contains an apostrophe (e.g. *who's, don't, it's*) you don't join the letters before and after it – you need to break instead.
  Show Me Children copy the punchline of the joke.

Big Book page 32

Independent work

Watch while children copy the joins. ❶
Check that all the joins are secure, and ask children to repeat any which appear shaky.

Encourage the children to read the instruction. ❷
Watch while they write the joke.

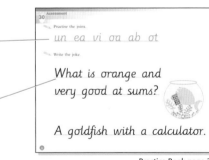
Practice Book page 32

❸
Children can use the assessment criteria on page 31 of the Practice Book to assess their own writing.

Take away

For additional practice of all the joins covered so far use **PCM 30**.

UNIT 1 How to join in a word: high-frequency words

1

Name .... Date ....

Read and then join the words.

the the the

what what

who

that

them

UNIT 2 Introducing the break letters: *j, g, x, y, z, b, f, p, q, r, s*

2

Name .... Date ....

Join the words – watch out for the break letters.

blue blue fawn

purple gold

jade yellow

soft aqua

blazing red

Name _____ Date _____

Trace and copy the patterns. Say the sounds.

eet   *eek*   *eel*

Finish the words, then copy them.

sw _____

ch _____

h _____

str _____

Name _____ Date _____

Trace and copy the patterns. Say the sounds.

ame   *ace*

Write the rhyming words, then copy them.

came		race	
n		sp	
g		l	
s		p	
t		pl	

3

4

Practising diagonal join, no ascender, to an anticlockwise letter in words: *ice, ide*

Name .... Date ....

Trace and copy the patterns. Say the sounds.

ice   *ice*

ide   *ide*

Write the rhyming words, then copy them.

mice	
r	
tw	
sp	
pr	

slide	
pr	
r	
gl	
h	

Practising horizontal join, no ascender, in words: *ow, ou*

Name .... Date ....

Read the limerick. Circle then write all the *ow* and *ou* words.

A mouse woke the proud Mrs Dowd.

She was frightened and screamed very loud.

A happy thought hit her,

To scare off the critter,

She sat up in bed and miaowed.

....

....

Practising horizontal join, no ascender, in words: *oy, oi*

Name _____ Date _____

Trace and copy the patterns. Say the sounds.

oy

oi

Finish the words.

t _____ ann   c _____ n   _____ l

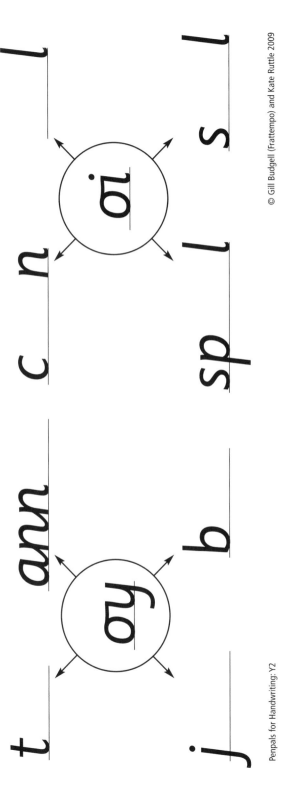

j _____ b   sp _____ l   _____ s

Practising horizontal join, no ascender, to an anticlockwise letter in words: *oa, ode*

Name _____ Date _____

Trace and copy the patterns. Say the sounds.

oa

ode

Finish the words, then copy them.

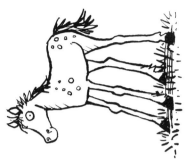
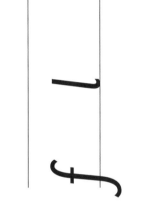

c _____ t   r _____ _____

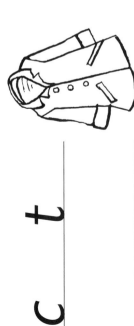

c _____   f _____ l

Practising horizontal join to ascender in words: *ole, obe*

Name .... Date ....

Trace and copy the patterns. Say the sounds.

ole

obe

Write the words, then copy them.

mole			robe		
v			str		
st			wardr		
h			gl		
wh			l		

Practising horizontal join to ascender in words: *ook, ool*

Name .... Date ....

Trace and copy the patterns. Say the sounds.

ook

ool

Trace and copy the patterns. Say the sounds.

Finish the words, then copy them.

b .... h ....

b .... p ....

sch ....

11

UNIT 11 Practising diagonal join to r: *ir, ur, er*

Name

Date

Trace and copy the patterns. Say the sound.

ir   *ur*   *er*

Finish the words, then copy them.

g   l   broth

ch   ch   p se

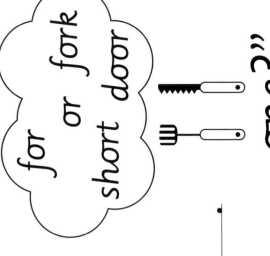

UNIT 12 Practising horizontal join to r: *or, oor*

Name

Date

Trace and copy the patterns. Say the sounds.

or   *oor*

Choose the words, then write them.

for   or   fork
short   door

"What's _____ tea?"

Knife and _____ .

Please close the _____ .

"A long one a _____ one."

Name _____ Date _____

Trace and copy the patterns. Say the sounds.

url   *irl*   *irt*

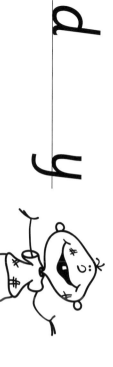

Finish the words, then copy them.

d __ y   sh __

c __ y   g __

Name _____ Date _____

Trace and copy the pattern. Say the sound.

ere

Finish the words, then copy them.

h __ th __ wh __

somewh __ anywh __

UNIT 15 Practising joining to and from r: *air*

Name _____ Date _____

Trace and copy the pattern. Say the word.

air   *air*

_____

Do the word sums.

p + *air* = _____

ch + *air* = _____

h + *air* = _____ + y = _____

f + *air* = _____ + y = _____

UNIT 16 Introducing diagonal join to s: *dis*

Name _____ Date _____

Trace and copy the patterns. Say the sounds.

is   *is*

dis   *dis*

Write the opposites.   *brother* _____

hers _____

like _____

agree _____

UNIT 17 Introducing horizontal join to s: *ws*

Name .... Date ....

Trace and copy the pattern. Say the sound.

ws ws

Sort and copy the words.

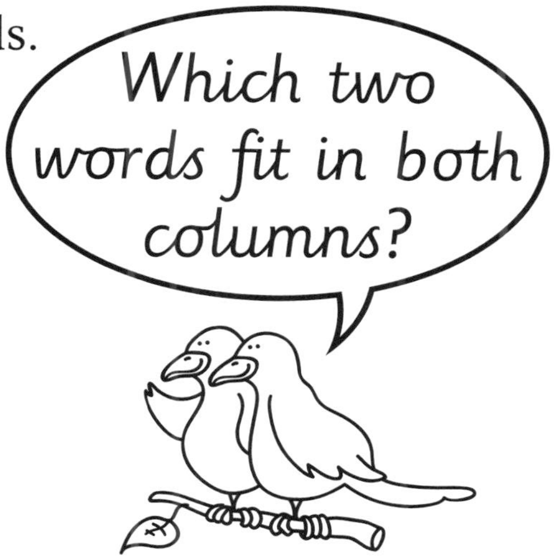

Which two words fit in both columns?

sounds like	**sounds like**
cows	grows

windows rows crows
shows eyebrows bows

UNIT 18 Introducing diagonal join from s to ascender: *sh*

Name .... Date ....

Trace and copy the pattern. Say the sound.

sh sh

Finish the words.
Choose one of the *sh* words and write it in each space.

pu and
spli and
scream and
could and

should
shout
splash
shove

Introducing diagonal join from s, no ascender: *si, su, se, sp, sm*

Name

Date

Trace and copy the patterns. Say the sounds.

si su se sp sm

Write two words which begin with each letter pattern.

si _____   *se* _____   *su* _____

_____   _____   _____

sm _____   *sp* _____

_____   _____

© Gill Budgell (Frattempo) and Kate Ruttle 2009

Introducing horizontal join from r to an anticlockwise letter: *rs*

Name

Date

Trace and copy the pattern.

rs rs

Choose one of the *rs* words and write it in each space.

| of course |
| doors |
| Morse |
| Mrs |

Mr and _____ Park

It's mine, _____

Close the _____

It's _____ code.

© Gill Budgell (Frattempo) and Kate Ruttle 2009

Name .... Date ....

Trace and copy the patterns. Say the sounds.

ea   *ear*

Sort and copy the words. Add one more in each column.

sounds like	**sounds like**
hear	*head*

fear   bread
tread   near
clear   dear
spread
thread

21

Name .... Date ....

Trace and copy the patterns. Say the sounds.

ft   *ft*

Sort and copy the words. Think of one more for each group.

after   fly
loft   flap
left   flan
often   flare

22

Introducing horizontal join from f, no ascender: *fu, fr*

Name _____ Date _____

Trace and copy the patterns. Say the sounds.

fu   *fr*

Read the sentence. Circle all the *fu* and *fr* patterns.

My frantic friend is full of fun and frolics.

Now write the sentence.

_____

Penpals for Handwriting: Y2

Introducing *qu* (diagonal join, no ascender)

Name _____ Date _____

Trace and copy the pattern. Say the sound.

qu   *qu*

Finish the words, then copy them.

qu ___ een   _____

qu ___ ick   _____

squ ___ arters   _____

squ ___ irrel   _____

Penpals for Handwriting: Y2

UNIT 25 Introducing *rr* (horizontal join, no ascender)

Name _____ Date _____

Trace and copy the pattern. Say the sound.

Read the sentence. Circle all the *rr* patterns.

Harry put the marrow on the barrow and then he was arrested.

Now write the sentence.

25

UNIT 26 Introducing *ss* (diagonal join, no ascender, to an anticlockwise letter)

Name _____ Date _____

ss *ss*

Trace and copy the pattern. Say the sound.

Finish and copy the words.

cro		hi	ed
pa		fu	ed
hi		pa	ed
a	ist	mi	ing

26

Name

Date

Trace and copy the pattern. Say the sound.

ff

Finish and copy the words.

hu____ → pu____

____ ff ____

di__erent

o____ er____ → stu____

o____

Name

Date

Look, say, cover, write and check the days of the week.

Make sure that capital letters are the same height as ascenders.

Monday

Saturday

Remember that *t* is a little bit shorter.

Monday	
Tuesday	
Wednesday	
Thursday	
Friday	
Saturday	
Sunday	

Name .... Date ....

Choose a piece of your own handwriting.

Read the statements and fill in the table.

Practise any joins you need to improve.

	YES	NO
1 The letters are all formed correctly.		
2 The letters all rest on the line, except for the descenders which hang below it.		
3 The small letters are all the same size.		
4 Ascenders and descenders are the same length.		
5 Capital letters are not joined. They are the same height as ascenders.		
6 Diagonal joins are all made correctly.		
7 Horizontal joins are all made correctly.		
8 Break letters (*b, p, g, j, x, y, z*) are not joined.		
9 Joins to and from *r, s* and *f* are all made correctly.		
10 The writing is clear and easy to read.		

Name .... Date ....

Trace the name and address.   Write your own name and address.

Miss E Prince,

24, Teezy Street,

Farwell,

Bertshire,

BY1 9GX

ABCDEFGHIJKLMNOPQRSTUVWXYZ

Penpals for Handwriting © Gill Budgell (Frattempo) and Kate Ruttle 2009

for right-handers

Penpals
writing mat

abcdefghijklmnopqrstuvwxyz

a b c d e f g h i j k l m n o p q r s t u v w x y z

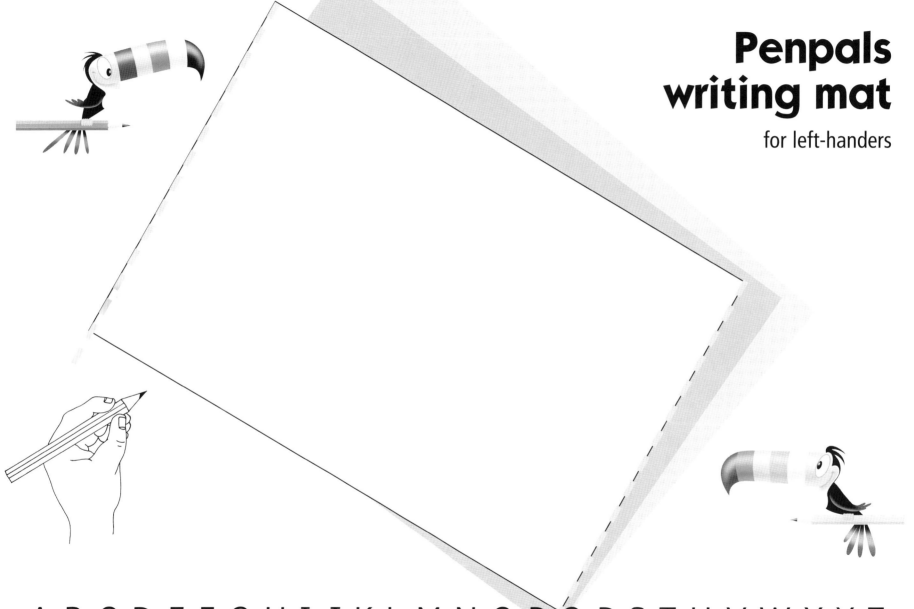

Penpals writing mat

for left-handers

A B C D E F G H I J K L M N O P Q R S T U V W X Y Z